Strategies of growth

The 'growth-share' matrix has dominated much recent thinking about business strategy and marketing, often over-simplifying the problems managers face and ignoring the needs of low-growth enterprises. This is a book about strategic choices. The author draws together competing theories on strategy, marketing and competitiveness and relates them to the needs of different types of enterprises in the real world beyond the classroom.

The result is an innovative approach to key issues in maturity, internationalization and corporate recovery that will be essential reading for those who need a fuller understanding of business strategy. Relating theory to current practice and to contemporary examples from around the world, the author has important lessons to offer, both for high-growth and low-growth enterprises. His book opens up the debate about corporate strategy in a way that will radically recast much current thinking about management decision making.

Alongside other titles in the *Routledge Series in Analytical Management*, this is an essential tool for today's manager and MBA student who need to break out of the comfortable orthodoxies and address the real problems facing managers in the fiercely competitive conditions of the 1990s.

Peter McKiernan is Senior Lecturer in Strategic Management and Group Convenor of the Marketing and Strategy Group at Warwick Business School, where he is also directing the full-time MBA programme. He is the co-author of *Sharpenders: Secrets of Unleashing Corporate Potential* (Blackwell 1988).

The Routledge series in analytical management
Series editor: David C. Wilson
University of Warwick

This series is a welcome new resource for advanced undergraduate and post-experience students of management who have lost patience with 'off the shelf' recipes for the complex problems of strategic change. Individual series titles cross-reference with each other in a thoroughly integrated approach to the key ideas and debates in modern management. The series will be essential reading for all those involved with studying and managing the individual, corporate and strategic problems of management change.

Other titles available in the series

A Strategy of Change
Concepts and controversies in the management of change
David C. Wilson

Technology and Organization
Power, meaning and design
Harry Scarbrough and J. Martin Corbett

Forthcoming

Competitiveness and Chaos
Walter Dean and Richard Whipp

Managing Culture
David Cray and Geoffrey Mallory

What is Strategy and Does it Matter?
Richard Whittington

Strategies of growth

Maturity, recovery and
internationalization

Peter McKiernan

London and New York

First published 1992
by Routledge
11 New Fetter Lane, London EC4P 4EE

Simultaneously published in the USA and Canada
by Routledge
a division of Routledge, Chapman and Hall, Inc.
29 West 35th Street, New York, NY 10001

© 1992 Peter McKiernan

Typeset by Leaper & Gard Ltd, Bristol, England
Printed and bound in Great Britain by
Mackays of Chatham PLC, Chatham, Kent

British Library Cataloguing in Publication Data
McKiernan, Peter
    Strategies of growth: maturity, recovery
    and internationalization
    I. Title
    658.4012

ISBN 0–415–07383–9
ISBN 0–415–05677–2 (pbk)

Library of Congress Cataloging in Publication Data
McKiernan, Peter
    Strategies of growth: maturity, recovery, and
    internationalization/Peter McKiernan
    (The Routledge series in analytical management)
    Includes bibliographical references and index
    1. Strategic planning   2. Corporate planning   I. Title
    II. Series
    HD30.28.M3845   1992
    658.4'012—dc20

ISBN 0–415–07383–9 (hb)   0–415–05677–2 (pbk)

Contents

Figures

Tables

Foreword

The field of strategic management is one which has seen a steady growth in its knowledge base, incorporating theories and research findings broadly from economics, business policy, organization theory and marketing. This has inevitably led towards the subject becoming inter-disciplinary. It has also led towards a degree of stultification. In many models of strategy formulation, complex patterns of strategies have become classified into typologies, each with its attendant set of management guides for decision making. In this book, McKiernan takes one such typology, the growth-share matrix, and subjects its assumptions and normative statements to analytical scrutiny. He finds that contrary to much received wisdom in the use of the matrix, many alternative strategies appear open to managers and organizations beyond those pronounced in the matrix. This is a book about strategic choices.

In the unfolding tradition of this series of books, the author's approach is one of uncovering the basic underlying assumptions of our knowledge base so far. Examining strategies in maturity, recovery and internationalization, McKiernan argues for a return to analytical approaches rather than relying on the creation and adoption of classificatory approaches which can stifle and suffocate the consideration of alternative strategies. This is an essential book for those managers and students of organization who wish to see beyond the normativism of much strategic management – who wish to understand organizational strategies rather than to view them as techniques to be applied in appropriate circumstances.

David C. Wilson
University of Warwick, 1991

Acknowledgements

The author and publishers would like to thank the following for the use of material in this book:

Heinemann Professional Publishers for permission to reproduce Figures 1.7, 1.8, 1.9, 1.10, 1.11, 1.12 from R. Walker 'Analysing the business portfolio in Black and Decker Europe', in B. Taylor and J. Harrison (1990) (eds) *The Manager's Casebook of Business Strategy*, Oxford: Heinemann.

Pergamon Press for permission to reproduce: Figures 3.6 and 3.7 from M. Perlitz (1985) 'Country portfolio analysis: assessing country risk and opportunity', *Long Range Planning* 18 (4): 11–16; and Table 4.8 from S.J.Q. Robinson (1986) 'Strategies for declining industrial markets', *Long Range Planning* 19 (2): 72–8.

Prentice Hall for permission to reproduce Figures 1.4 and 1.13 from A. Hax and N.S. Majluf (1984) *Strategic Management: An Integrated Perspective*, Englewood Cliffs, NJ.: Prentice Hall.

Finally, while every reasonable effort has been made to obtain permission for use of the material cited, the publishers would like to apologise for any inadvertent omissions.

Abbreviations

ADL	Arthur D. Little
BCG	Boston Consulting Group
BD	Black & Decker
CEO	chief executive officer
CPI	company potential for internationalization
DC	developing countries
DCF	discounted cash flow
DGI	degree of globality of the industry
ELS	effective low-share business
FDI	foreign direct investment
GBV	gross book value
GDP	gross domestic product
GE	General Electric Company
GI	General Instrument Company
GNP	gross national product
IDR	investment depreciation ratio
ILS	ineffective low-share business
LDC	less developed countries
MMM	Minnesota Mining and Manufacturing Company
MNC	multinational company
MNE	multinational enterprise
NIC	newly industrialized country
NPV	net present value
OBR	operating pattern, beliefs and rules
OECD	Organization for Economic Co-operation and Development
OEM	original equipment manufacturing (er)
OIS	online information services
OPEC	Organization of Petroleum Exporting Countries

PIMS	profit impact of marketing strategy
PLC	product life cycle
RCF	rate of cash flow
ROI	return on investment
SBU	strategic business unit
SME	small and medium-sized enterprise
SWOT	strength, weakness, opportunity, threat
TI	Tube Investments
WIC	Western industrialized country

Introduction

It is not difficult to develop a creeping form of blindness in academia. Levitt (1960) referred to a myopia that limits marketing vision. In many instances this visual distortion is caused by the ready availability or ubiquitous presence of a new tool or technique of analysis. In the 1960s and 1970s the advent of econometric techniques took a feverish grip on economists. Academic journals were subsequently swamped with a plethora of empirical analyses accompanied by coefficients of determination (R^2) on fit and Durbin-Watson statistics on autocorrelation. The quality of some of this early analysis yielded a disparate array of results from which few generalizable conclusions could be drawn. Only now, with careful method, are some of the key relationships being unravelled.

Marketeers and strategists are also guilty. The best-known and most widely taught portfolio planning technique is the growth-share matrix, or more crudely, the 'Boston Box'. From its true origins in the 1960s through its development in the 1970s, it has become the primary portfolio method for simplifying the analysis of a spread of business (or product)[1] mixes. Its cash generating cows plough money into question-mark businesses facilitating their movement into the star category. Markets mature as growth slows and the stars become cash cows. The process is a continuous one. The movement of cash between the three 'major' cells prompts associated strategies: *harvest* the cows; *build* the question-mark businesses; *hold* the stars. The focus is on balancing interests in three 'major' cells. This is how to win. The message is shouted loud and clear to motivated MBA students and senior management. It is rarely questioned, except perhaps by the most perceptive of undergraduates unshackled by empirical experience.

Therein lies the myopia or creeping blindness. If 80 per cent of businesses lie in the dog category (McNamee 1988), what options do managers pursue? The automatic prescriptive strategy suggested by the growth-share matrix for this cell is 'divestment'. This is a sad indictment for a technique which, after all, is a powerful pedagogic aid. The growth-share matrix is not meant to be so restrictive of strategy choice. Unfortunately, the uncritical and uncreative manner in which it is taught can readily lead the unwary to this conclusion. Moreover, its rapid spread among, and strong adoption by, board policy advisers and executives with strategic decision-making powers has created an empirical, in addition to an academic, myopia. Strategy formulation has concentrated mainly on the three 'major' cells and become unnecessarily restricted in the fourth 'forgotten' cell. Morrison and Wensley (1991) have recently referred to this unfortunate side-effect of the growth-share matrix as a 'boxing in' of strategic discussions to a limited set of options and prescriptions.

Clearly, divestment is not the only strategic course in the 'forgotten cell'. Organizational examples provide a rich array of case evidence indicating the successful pursuance of other strategies. In addition, academic scholars[2] have provided rigorous research results, documenting the wider adoption of other strategies in the 'forgotten cell'. In the correct context, divestment may well be the preferred and desirable option. But there will be many contexts in which superior options exist. Options that can turn dogs into question marks, stars or cows.

The impact of the terminology, though, cannot be under-estimated. Operational executives on management development programmes commonly use the term dog in a condescending manner. Porter (1985) refers colourfully to the horrified expression on the faces of managers when you explain that the business under their care is a dog. Dogs are not good businesses to be associated with. They are a drain on time. It is far more rewarding to be winning market share. Hence the attitude prevails that dog businesses should be divested.

There is an alternative and more positive stance. The majority of businesses are not dogs. The original BCG matrix referred to them as mortgages (a large cash flow but no growth). Mortgages are convertible and flexible. There are many examples of dog businesses, which, once divested, often thrive for years under more entrepreneurial, efficient or effective managements – particularly with an ownership incentive e.g. management by-out/by-ins. Hence, there must be alternative strategies to divestment in the 'forgotten cell'.

This book concentrates on the 'forgotten cell', examining three key alternative strategies. First, as mortgages can be converted, so too can businesses be transformed. The recovery literature provides insights into corporate rejuvenation. This is examined in a critical way, spelling out the general lessons. How organizations manage the change process from decline through recovery to a superior position in their market/industry (however defined). Second, mortgages do not have to be constrained by the domestic limitations on the size of their markets. International mortgages can be the key to expansion. How, why and under what conditions do organizations successfully achieve an international presence? Finally, mortgages can have long and profitable lives. Organizations in low-growth markets/industries or with low market shares in their markets/industries can achieve sound long-term postures. What do they do that is different?

The three alternative strategies presented for the 'forgotten cell' are not exhaustive as a classification. Neither are they mutually exclusive. They can, and do, occur in combinations. These combinations can even include divestment as a 'shaping' or enabling strategy. Moreover, their use is not confined to the 'forgotten cell'. Internationalization strategies can be utilized in question-mark businesses and the secrets of corporate recovery can equally well apply to cash-cow businesses. But the message that they all apply to low-growth, low-share 'forgotten cell' businesses is the theme of this book. The aim of this book is to explore the strategic choices open to those who look beyond the 'boxed' classification of strategies.

Initially, however, we concentrate on the growth-share matrix. It is set in its true historical context, its advantages and disadvantages are described. Both valid and invalid criticisms are examined. Its development and the parallel development of similar portfolio techniques is appraised in a sequential manner. Current usage of these techniques points to the dominance of the growth share matrix. This heralds the suggestion of myopia. Consequently, the alternative options to divestment are examined – strategies for recovery and rejuvenation (strategies for internationalization) and strategies for low-share and low-growth businesses.

Chapter 1

Strategy formulation and the growth-share matrix

INTRODUCTION

The extraordinary trading boom after 1945 forced many American companies to adjust their business planning systems. There was a movement away from the dominance of budgeting and financial control which provided only short-run projection (typically 1 year). Capacity expansions to meet the boom, together with their financing, made it necessary to increase the horizons for these projections. Consequently, long-range planning techniques evolved which defined objectives, goals, policies, programmes and budgets spreading over a much longer time period. These were guiding policy frameworks, designed to focus managerial efforts on more precise objectives. Consequently, the degree of formality in business planning increased. The advent of capital budgeting and with it the use of discounted cash flows (DCF) and pay-back periods to evaluate capital-expenditure programmes introduced a sophistication in technique not witnessed in the previous budgetary days.

Unfortunately, for both internal and external reasons, long-range planning became a frustrating activity. Internally, many planning systems involved no more than a historic extrapolation of sales trends. There was little attention paid to wider environmental (economic, demographic, social, legal, technological) changes and operating market characteristics (competitor reaction, entry and exit barriers, power of customers and suppliers) and how these elements would alter naïve forecasting projections. Small wonder that historic sales projections rarely equated with actual results. Without a well developed analysis of variance to examine the difference, managers became annoyed and frustrated with the continuous failure of this practice.

Externally, the relatively quiet conditions of high market growth, predictable trends, dominant single-business firms and limited competition that, initially, were essential for the successful spread and operation of forecasting techniques began to change. Growth started to stabilize in the 1960s inducing greater competitor reactions in markets and industries as companies fought to retain or to increase market shares as market size levelled off. In addition, the dominant single business was beginning to fragment into separate business units with the autonomy to develop their own strategies. The classic example is that of the American company General Electric (GE) which in 1970, was broken down from a corporation specializing in electric motors and lighting into a conglomerate of strategic business units (SBUs) with interests across industrial segments.

Traditional long-range planning techniques cannot easily cope with environmental turbulence which directly limits forecasting accuracy. Nor can their functional orientation handle a spread of business interests, each with its own needs for development. Moreover, the focus on individual projects on a case by case basis (e.g. using DCF techniques) ignores the overall corporate portfolio and its development. Project(s) may well have to proceed in specific SBUs to maintain the balance of the corporate whole, no matter what the result of the individual DCF-based decision is. Management of a portfolio of businesses is distinctly different from that of a single dominant business. It requires different planning techniques. These were soon to evolve.

In the latter part of the 1960s and throughout the 1970s a collection of portfolio planning techniques was developed to assist managers in the running of diversified businesses in complex environments. The development of the two major techniques happened in parallel (Schoeffler et al. 1974). The General Electric Company, who, taking advice from the consultants McKinsey and Co. had broken their dominant business into separate SBUs, were already well advanced in the development and use of corporate planning techniques in the early 1970s. They initiated a portfolio matrix approach to help manage the spread of these SBUs. This approach (which will be examined in detail later) was paralleled by the development of the growth-share matrix by the Boston Consulting Group (BCG). This simple four-cell matrix quickly gained widespread appeal and use, both in the business and the academic worlds.

This chapter has two main objectives. First, to reinforce the argument in the introductory chapter that the automatic prescriptive strategy of 'divestment' is not the only one available in the 'forgotten cell'. What other things can we do with the dogs? Second, it addresses the nature of use of the growth-share matrix, emphasizing its first-phase analytical role and illustrating how to use it safely. Throughout this book the unit of analysis is the organization. The growth-share matrix is equally useful at the product level. Clearly much of the commentary will apply at this level but readers are drawn to the early debates (see Abell and Hammond 1979) on the sensitivity of the matrix to the unit of analysis under discussion.

PRECURSORS OF THE GROWTH-SHARE MATRIX

The BCG was formed in 1963 by Bruce Henderson. It was generally regarded as the pioneer of business strategy analysis (Lorange 1975). In fact, as early as 1964 Henderson advised his clients that long-range planning should not be equated with 5-year budgets; strategic thinking was required to compete and minimize the changing general and operating environments that businesses found themselves in during the 1960s.

The development of the now famous growth-share matrix was evolutionary. It depended on the independent formulation of two ideas – the 'experience curve' and the 'sustainable growth formula'.

Experience curve

In Henderson's[1] own words:

> As far as I know, I originated the idea of the Experience Curve in the late 1960s. The idea first started when I was doing work for the Norton Company who were competing with the Minnesota Mining and Manufacturing Company (MMM) in industrial tapes. I noticed that the price was constantly going down if the effects of inflation were removed. I also noticed that Norton's costs had been going down in parallel with the price. MMM's market share was several times that of Norton and it has apparently a very profitable product line for MMM, but a loser for Norton. That could have been because of scale effects, but that did not explain why the cost was going down in such a very consistent pattern for both competitors.
>
> (Henderson 1988)

This is important. The statement highlights the rapid decline in costs but suggests that falling production costs alone (scale effects) may not be the only cause. Much work had been done in the 1950s, using the engineering approach, to analyse plant scale economies. The pioneer was Joe Bain (1956) at Harvard. His classic text and its findings would have been known to practising strategy consultants during the 1960s, especially those consultants (e.g. BCG) based in the same city. Falling production costs with scale were well understood. During the 1960s, as growth rates stabilized, there was a shift in emphasis by businesses away from production to marketing. Excess demand, that had guaranteed sales for manufactured goods in the 1950s, was drying up. Business had to try and sell its output, and marketing was the new discipline for this. Consequently, compared with previous decades, marketing and associated administration costs were rising in corporations just as Henderson was pursuing his assignments.

At this time, BCG examined the electronic components manufacturing interests of the General Instrument Company as colour television began to enter the market. Henderson found that the cost of the triple-yoke elements for colour TV was declining faster than the single yokes had done in the growth of monochrome TV. As Bain's Harvard research had shown, this trend was not new. Soon after the GI assignment, Henderson discovered an article on the manufacture of fighter planes during the Second World War. When man hours were plotted against the number of planes built, the precise pattern that Henderson had witnessed at GI was traced out. Significantly, this curve plotted a straight line on log-log co-ordinates if the vertical axis was man hours per plane and the horizontal axis was the cumulative number of planes built. In other words the number of hours required dropped by a constant percentage each time the total number of planes produced doubled. Henderson, writing in 1988, recalls:

A few months later, I was given an urgent and seemingly impossible assignment by General Instrument. They had just hired a number of scientists who had been at the leading edge of the development of the then new technology of MOS semiconductors. GI was already in the semiconductor business, but not a leader in the field. They wanted to know what the prices would be on semiconductors over the next 10 years. That would be a real guessing game unless some characteristic pattern could be found that had some supporting logic except chance. Our case team was able to use the trade association to get price indices and volumes of output for many categories of electronic components. To our delight we found that there was a characteristic pattern in those prices when the inflation was removed and they were plotted on log-log coordinates. *That was when the Experience Curve was born.*

Where the definition of the product was consistent enough over time, BCG found this pattern evolved on most assignments. The implication was not only that prices had fallen because costs had fallen, but those who accumulated most experience seemed to have lower costs than those who had accumulated less experience. The experience-curve effect was novel. Unlike the learning curve it encompasses all costs – capital, administration, research and *marketing*, and has a 'transferred impact from one product to another through the process of technological displacement and produce evolution.'[2] The rising marketing costs of the time were readily incorporated into the construct. Henderson concluded that:

> If cost is a reciprocal function of total experience then cost is also a function of *market share*.[3] Those products in which a competitor has a large market share should be expected to be those in which he has a competitive advantage in cost. Those companies which are growing faster than the competition should be increasing their competitive advantage as a consequence.

Sustainable growth formula

The second fundamental idea in the development of the growth-share matrix was the sustainable growth formula. In the early 1970s, another BCG consultant, Alan Zakon, was helping the Mead Paper Corporation[4] to develop strategies for each of its diversified SBUs (6 product groups and 45 operating divisions). As a former finance professor he was keen on the notion of 'net free cash flow'. In all businesses this must be kept positive. The paper business at Mead, although having growth potential, was a large consumer of cash. Zakon extended his development of the idea of 'cash deficient' and 'growth deficient' businesses while analysing the Mead businesses (for the BCG). There was a need for a balance between cash generators and cash users if growth was to be funded. Growth requires the use of significant cash investments over an extended time frame before the business can achieve a positive net cash flow and return funds back to the group. This relationship was known as the sustainable growth formula. As Henderson (1988) states: 'It effectively integrates the effects of debt, interest rates, dividend rates, tax rates, return on equity and growth in equity as a result of the rate of return on equity.'

So the companies with the highest returns can, theoretically, be the fastest growers. Zakon's idea is simply a maximum rate of growth that a firm can achieve by using its internal financial resources and debt capacity.[5]

From the Mead experience, together with inputs from other BCG financial experts, Zakon was able to develop a matrix representing the flows of cash. Figure 1.1 depicts the original four-cell matrix. It consists of *bonds* (where there is a steady cash flow from interest and capital growth); *savings accounts* (where there is no cash flow but compound growth); *mortgages* (where there is a large cash flow but no growth); *sweepstakes*[6] (similar to venture capital opportunities). As Morrison and Wensley (1991) state:

> Hence was born the first form of the Boston Box without any specific axes and presented solely as a taxonomy device. It contained no value judgements about attractive or unattractive quadrants but merely recognized the need for some balance between the categories.

It directly considered the sustainable growth rate for the company as a function of its portfolio of cash-generating and cash-using businesses.

FORMATION OF THE GROWTH-SHARE MATRIX

To form the growth-share matrix, Zakon's maximum sustainable growth rate had now to be linked to the experience curve. It was Henderson, in open discussion about Zakon's matrix within BCG, who provided the bridging mechanism. If the company with the highest returns can grow the fastest (a logical deduction from Zakon's work) and the company with the highest market share has the highest profit margin (a logical deduction from Henderson's work) then the latter should be able to finance the highest growth rate. When this rate stabilizes the net positive cash flows can be used to finance business in low market share positions that have a potential for rapid growth. The Zakon–Henderson nexus was complete. The box was born.

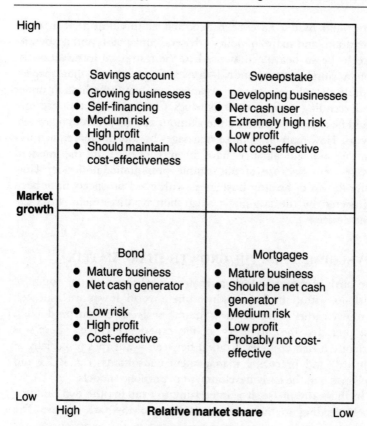

High

Market growth

Low

Savings account	Sweepstake
• Growing businesses	• Developing businesses
• Self-financing	• Net cash user
• Medium risk	• Extremely high risk
• High profit	• Low profit
• Should maintain cost-effectiveness	• Not cost-effective

Figure 1.1 Mead Corporation original matrix
Source: Francis J. Aguilar, *The Mead Corporation: Strategic Planning*, Boston: Harvard Business School, Case 0-379-070

The birth was a quiet affair: a simple box showing growth plotted against market share with no grids and no value-laden categories. It was purely a presentational device, as Zakon had used this matrix to communicate his ideas to the Mead Board. Henderson (1988), who was later guilty of some extravagant claims[7] for the growth-share matrix is surprisingly humble about its origins at Mead: 'The Boston Box is nothing more than the interaction in a single company of the finances of products (or SBUs) which have differing growth rates and also have differing market shares.'

It could hardly have been expected at this time that a whole generation (and more) of policy advisers, consultants and academics were to be so heavily influenced in their strategy formulation by such a simple presentational device. So much so, that specific, credible strategic options for organizations would be hidden under condescending category titles like dogs. On the other hand, pressure would be created to push for the glamour category, through growth, of stars. How many misplaced marriages by way of merger, acquisition or strategic alliance have been conceived in the modern business era because of this simple presentational device? How many deaths of healthy businesses with good prospects have been engineered by the automatic suggestion of 'divestment' from the same device?

DEVELOPMENT OF THE GROWTH-SHARE MATRIX

The birth of the growth-share matrix owed much to the notion of portfolios within the financial investment world. It was also indebted to much earlier work on cost/volume scale effects on production that preceded the 'discovery' of the experience curve. There was evidently a rich cross-fertilization between academics (especially at Harvard) and practising management consultants (e.g. BCG and McKinsey) in the early development of portfolio models.

In this early phase, it is interesting to examine the two building blocks leading to the creation of the growth-share matrix. The production scale economies incorporated in the experience-curve platform related, in the main, to observations in a single dominant business. That is, after all, where mainstream scale economies lie. However, the sustainable-growth argument rested on the relationship between cash-deficient and cash-generating businesses. It was 'borrowed' from portfolio work in financial investment theory and was most suitable for the analysis of diversity or spread within a group of businesses. Moreover, in the translation to the growth-share matrix, the risk-return relationship at the root of Markowitz's (1952) financial portfolio theory was, significantly, lost. However, the former argument rests heavily on the attainment of market share in single dominant businesses in order to become a low-cost producer. Hence the growth-share matrix has built on blocks representing both single dominant businesses and diversified ones. It could be argued that the growth-share matrix was ill-conceived in the first instance, i.e. it was a mongrel type of 'dog' itself.

From these early origins, the growth-share matrix developed incrementally, to the much used (abused?) device so commonly found in marketing and strategy textbooks.[8] This development had two stages.

Stage 1

The Zakon matrix underwent a process of development within BCG such that, by 1970, the categories on the new presentational device had a familiar ring to them (see Figure 1.2).

1   *Bonds become cash cows*: these were businesses with relatively high market shares in low-growth markets. They had strong positive 'net cash flows' accruing from their volume sales output, via experience curve effects, to a low-cost producer position. Moreover, costs were additionally reduced by the lack of competition, which had depleted given the powerful position of the cash cow and the general unattractive nature of the market. It is the excess cash flows generated which can then be ploughed, Zakon fashion, into cash-deficient businesses in the group.

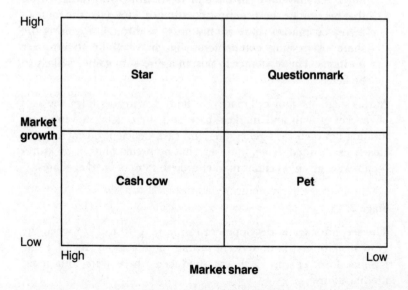

Figure 1.2 Stage 1: development of the growth-share matrix

2   *Savings accounts become stars*: stars have a high relative market
     share in a high growth market. They can be either cash-
     generating or cash-deficient businesses. The possibility of large
     net cash flows is offset by funds needed to maintain their
     position in the face of strong competition. If stars are best placed
     within the portfolio to carry the future of the group, they can
     attract increasing amounts of cash as strategists attempt to guar-
     antee their future as cash cows. The alternative is to allow them
     to slip back into the question-mark category.

3   *Sweepstakes became question marks*: what do you do with products
     or businesses in high-growth markets with low market shares
     relative to competitors? The question marks were aptly named.
     At the development or growth stage of its life cycle, such a
     business requires substantial amounts of funding. The cash
     generators need to feed these cash-deficient businesses on a
     grand scale if they are going to accrue market share. The invest-
     ment, as in all financial portfolios, is risky. The question marks
     can be moved across to become stars or fall down to become
     pets.

4   *Mortgages become pets*: pets are nice to have around, largely for
     emotional reasons. They can represent modest negative cash
     flows yet may have an integral relationship with other SBUs
     that necessitate their continued existence. However, the route to
     increased market share is only possible through acquiring the
     share of existing competitors who may all be in stronger
     positions. The resistance to this, in a zero-sum game, is likely to
     be fierce.

At this stage, the four-cell matrix, its familiar category titles, the axes
of market growth and market share and the crucial movement of
funding between cash-generating and cash-deficient businesses was
clearly established. Note, however, that no breakpoints or measurements were given on either market-growth rates or market shares.

Stage 2

The second stage of development ran from 1970 to 1973 when the
growth-share matrix underwent further modifications. By 1973, the
familiar form (Figure 1.3) was produced. there were four main
modifications:

1   *Pets become dogs*: this change seemed not only unfortunate but

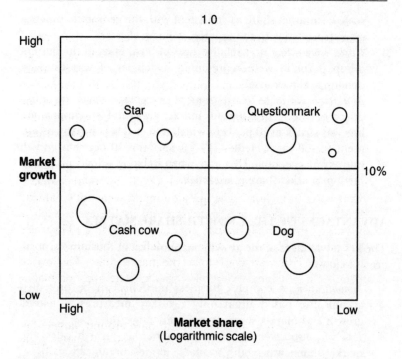

Figure 1.3 Stage 2: development of the growth-share matrix

discourteous. As Henderson (1973) points out, the BCG saw dogs as 'essentially worthless'. They should be liquidated in order that their accumulated hunger for cash from elsewhere does not damage the group irreparably. Groups must avoid this 'cash trap'. This simple, and at the time innocuous change, could have been singularly responsible for the subsequent myopia or 'boxing in' of strategic thought. Dogs can be destructive creatures and require a good deal of management time to exercise them. Perhaps this connotation permeated quicker and deeper into our strategic mentality than all the others taken together.

2   *Market share on a logarithmic scale*: earlier versions of the model portrayed a simple distinction between high and low market shares. There was an implicit assumption that market leadership distinguished between the two categories. The 1973 version was more explicit, tacking on relative market share and expressing this on a logarithmic scale. Hedley (1977) views this

scale for market share as consistent with the geometric progression associated with the experience-curve effects.

3 *Circles representing size*: relative sizes of businesses in the current group portfolio were represented by circles of various sizes, denoting sales or assets.

4 *Market growth in percentage terms*: a percentage scale was introduced on the vertical axis for market growth. The demarcation line was struck at 10 per cent which reflected 'a company investment cut-off rate'. Hedley (1977) views this 10 per cent growth rate as an acceptable DCF rate when inflation is low and investment in market share is attractive.

ADVANTAGES OF THE GROWTH-SHARE MATRIX

The key advantages of the growth-share matrix in this familiar form are as follows:

1 *Simplification*: a complex business portfolio can be presented graphically, based upon only two key measures – market growth and market share. It is visually powerful.

2 *Ease of construction*: information on market growth rates and market shares was readily available to most organizations.

3 *Classification*: businesses can be allocated to categories based upon their current capacity as cash-generating or cash-deficient units.

4 *Funding*: the investment required by members of each category of the portfolio can be estimated and cash-flow movements from cash generators to cash-deficient businesses can be planned.

5 *Balancing*: the cash-generating and cash-deficient businesses can be balanced to achieve a 'sustainable growth' portfolio.

6 *Strategic planning*: a construction of the matrix, no matter how detailed, helps managers to get started on the difficult route to strategy formulation. The matrix can help to mark out the underlying life cycle for businesses enabling the identification of 'success' and 'disaster' sequences (see Figure 1.4). Moreover, strategic options could be suggested by a cursory examination, e.g.

Category	*Strategy*
Cash cow	Hold or harvest
Stars	Hold

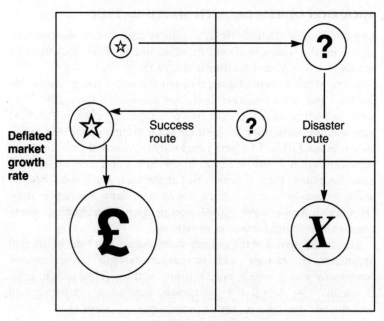

Figure 1.4 Strategic planning: success and disaster routes
Source: Adapted from Hax and Majluf (1984)

Dogs   Divest
Question marks Divest or invest heavily to build

7 *Competitive benchmarking*: the use of the growth-share matrix was
not limited to the management of an organization's own portfolio. With the ease of construction, due to readily available
corporate information in the USA and UK, portfolios could be
built up for direct competitors. A collection of these over time
gave an indication of competitor strategies. (Moreover, if the
individual competitor portfolios are constructed on clear acetate
sheets, a fast movement through the sheets in front of a slide
projector acts like a movie of strategic change, plotting out
competitor's moves and enabling a close reading of their respective strategies.)

ADOPTION OF THE GROWTH-SHARE MATRIX

The advantages, particularly in simplicity and ease of construction, facilitated the widespread and rapid adoption of the growth-share matrix in US corporations during the 1970s.

Some of these corporations, through the astute use of favourable tax laws and money-market debt, had grown to a large size. They were struggling with the strictures of long-range planning and, to increase flexibility, they broke their large groups down into quasi-autonomous SBUs. The new conglomerates needed new means of communication from the centre to the SBUs and new methods of co-ordination of their activities. But at the same time, the USA and world economy was becoming more turbulent. Oil price rises, creeping inflation and global competition was forcing many companies into tight financial situations.

Hence the arrival of the growth-share matrix at a time of internal organizational change and increasing external environmental complexity was a timely one. Various authors (Haspeslagh 1982; Bowman 1974; Ansoff 1984) illustrated how most companies had introduced the matrix under conditions of crisis and capital constraint, in situations of uncertainty and competitive pressure. By 1972, when the matrix was only 2 years old, it was being used by over a hundred major US companies (Day 1977); by 1975, it was universally practised as a method of analysis (Lorange 1975) and by 1978 was spread across a wide range of companies and industries. Moreover, it was being used as a fully integrated part of the corporate-planning process.

Its timely arrival was not the only reason for its rapid adoption. Authors have pointed to the intuitive appeal of matrices (Day 1977); the appetite of business managers for 'fashionable products' (Wilson and Atkin 1976); the cascade effect from large to small businesses (Bowman 1974); the parallel research findings of the Marketing Science Institute using the profit impact of marketing strategy (PIMS) database that confirmed the strong correlation between market share and profitability, 'validating' the growth-share matrix that relied on this linkage; the role of the Harvard Business School in disseminating the knowledge (with whom BCG were closely associated); and the prominence of BCG itself among top US corporations in a period of excess demand for consultancy services. As Morrison and Wensley (1991) show, it had all the properties that are empirically correlated with studies of rapid innovation in other products.

Clearly, business managers grasped the technique quickly and used it at a high level of analysis for strategic decision making. This finding contrasts with the attitude of the BCG. Although during the early stages of the wider adoption of its matrix in the 1970s, they shifted their emphasis on it away from a purely presentational device to a first-brush analysis of the understanding of the mutual dependencies of SBUs in multi-product businesses. (A first stage of analysis requires an understanding of the system dynamics of such organizations.) Henderson (1988) was adamant: 'It is a minor clue to the dynamics of cash flow in a multi-product organisation. That is all. I never thought of it as more than that.' The idea was considered (within BCG) 'as interesting and perhaps useful but certainly not a major tool for management'.

Wise words from the inventors. Their caution however, was not followed by many strategists in organizations or by the majority of academic teachers. By 1989, despite having a 100˙ per cent occupancy rate on management degree programmes among UK universities and institutions of further education, the growth-share matrix was only taught in a critical manner in 20 per cent of them. Yet during the 1970s and 1980s the academic world was particularly harsh in its criticism of the matrix and, more generally, of the 'new orthodoxy' of portfolio modelling.

ACTUAL AND PERCEIVED PROBLEMS WITH THE GROWTH-SHARE MATRIX

The following section describes the 'difficulties' and 'dangers' in constructing and using the growth-share matrix. At each stage, suggestions are given to aid the reader. The growth-share matrix has few, real disadvantages. However, there are 'difficulties' in the construction and operations of a simple tool in complex circumstances and 'dangers' inherent in its naive use.

At base, it is a presentational device. It seeks to encapsulate in four variables⁹ a strategic profile of a multi-business organization. In this form, acting as a first pass at understanding the underlying dynamics of the organization (as Henderson intended) it has no peers. For the era of internal and external change to which it was born, it was fully appropriate. The change in key contingency variables over time may have eroded the importance of growth and market share as corporate objectives. But it is arguable, even now, whether there is a simpler, more concise and more powerful means by which managers can begin to think in strategic terms about their spread of businesses. Yet the criticism has been intense. The only way to credibly examine this critique is to compare it with the original objective of the growth-share matrix – that of a first-pass analysis. In this form it is a tool. Unfortunately, it has grown to such a stature over the last two decades that even practitioners (Walker 1990) refer to it as a theory. It is not a theory and cannot, therefore, be placed on trial and faced with questions on refutability, consistency, comprehensiveness and so on. Academic discourse in this area is irrelevant and misplaced.

The range of criticisms directed at the growth-share matrix can be placed into three groups. First, there are those pertaining to 'difficulties' in its construction and operation. Second, there are those relating to the 'dangers' of naive and careless use. Finally, there are a group of 'damaging' criticisms, closely linked to the second, yet separated by an optimistic expectation of the matrix's capabilities and characterized by false analogy and an unfortunate, yet genuine, call for a re-focusing of attention on other variables.

Difficulties

Market definition and measurement

The fundamental difficulty with the growth-share matrix is the definition of the market for both the vertical (growth) and horizontal (share) axes.

In the 80 per cent of cases where it was taught uncritically on management courses in the UK (1989 Warwick Survey)[10] no respondents mentioned the crucial issue of market definition among the few problems they did identify. As Henderson (1988) emphasizes:

> In your own explanation of this subject you should pay particular attention to the real problems with Experience Curves and the 'Boston Box'. How do you define a product? How do you define a market? What is an automobile? What is a truck? What is the transportation market? ...
>
> Markets can be defined in many dimensions which include product differences, secondary attributes, image and customer characteristics and values. A trip [from the USA] to Europe may be the competitor of the new automobile. Both are part of the travel market.

Indeed poor market definition has been a strong academic criticism (Fruhan 1972; Wilson and Atkins 1986). Economists[11] have long grappled with market definitions on the demand side and with the distinguishing role of consumer substitution. Howe (1986) suggests that the analyst should adopt a definition of the market which embraces all products identified by consumers as substitutes. It must be remembered that the boundaries of the market will change as new substitutes appear or as the nature of the market segments change. The problem of definition is exacerbated by many Government sponsored statistics (especially in the UK) which are based on supply-side definitions of industries (e.g. minimum list headings).

Hence it is important when defining markets to take into account managerial and customer perceptions (i.e. managerial judgement) of what constitutes 'operating' markets. Real competition and decisions are, after all, based upon these judgements.

Market-share scale

In the development of the growth-share matrix the original categories of high and low market share on the horizontal axis were plotted onto a semi-log scale to reflect the underlying experience curve effects. There are two important issues.

First, the scale is a relative one, i.e. 'the business/products share of the market divided by the share of the next largest competitor'. A simple comparison between two firms A and Z with market shares of 25 and 35 per cent of their respective markets may yield an erroneous conclusion that Z is in the stronger position. A better assessment of their competitive positions (and the structure of their markets) is given by taking '*relative*' market share (actual market share divided by that of its next largest competitor). As the example in Table 1.1 shows, although firm Z has a superior actual market share (35 to 25 per cent) over firm A, it only has a relative market share of 0.9 (35 ÷ 40) compared to A with 1.7 (25 ÷ 15). A clear market leader in an industry will have a relative market share greater than 1. Joint industry leaders will score exactly 1.0.

Second, on the relative market-share scale the distinction between high and low share was originally set out as a relative market share of 1.0. This is based on Henderson's (1979) view that 'a stable competitive market never has more than three significant competitors, the largest of which has no more than four times the market share of the smallest!' Hence only the market leader has

Table 1.1 Actual and relative market shares for A, Z, and their competitors

	Market 1				Market 2			
	A	B	C	D	Z	Y	X	W
Actual	25	15	10	10	35	40	20	5
Relative	1.7	0.6	0.4	0.4	0.9	1.1	0.5	0.1

Source: Adapted from McNamee (1988), Chapter 7.

significant strength. However, it has been argued that in practice a share position of 1.0 (joint leaders) can be highly competitive and unprofitable (Walker 1989). Hence, after Hedley (1977) the line is usually drawn at 1.5, as positions better than this can more seriously be considered to be dominant.

Market-growth rates

The original specification of a 10 per cent growth rate has attracted criticism (Kotler 1984). The cut-off rate (or discount rate) is important as it will vary among firms and across industries. Hax and Majluf (1984) point out that, when all firms belong to the same industry, this cut-off point should be the average growth for that industry. The business position is then a relative one; above the line are embryonic or growth units and below it are mature ones.

The problem arises for conglomerate organizations operating in unrelated industries. If the units all have a common country base, the analyst could select a macroeconomic measure e.g. GDP growth. If the businesses are scattered internationally, it may be possible to use a weighted average of the growth rate of each individual business. A corporate growth target would also be a legitimate choice. Certainly Henderson and Hedley (both BCG) considered that 10 per cent was an acceptable discount rate when inflation was low and investment in market share was attractive. Moreover, no matter what cut-off rate is chosen, the measure must either consistently take inflation into account in the construction of the vertical scale and in the measurement of the cut-off rate (i.e. real terms) or it should contain them both in nominal terms.

Further academic criticism has focused on these cut-off rates together with the arbitrary nature of the scales, the criterion used for

cut-off points and the consequent variability of the resultant classification. Wind, Mahajan and Swire (1981) examined growth-share
classifications of 15 Fortune 500 companies using 4 different market
share and 4 different growth definitions. They showed that only 4
out of the 15 companies were consistently classified. This point is
reinforced by Goold (1981) and Majaro (1977).

Morrison and Wensley (1991) have recently argued that: 'these
classifications are the linchpin of the subsequent development of
mission statements and broad investment orientations, they are
potentially both valid and relevant criticisms'.

If the benchmark for testing the utility of this tool is its original
design purpose (presentational; first-phase analysis) it is difficult to
accept them as valid and relevant criticisms. First, the axis
constructs are sound enough. The pedantic critic may wish to
exploit the experience curve-based horizontal axis, in the sense that
it implicitly assumes a homogeneity of cost profiles among
companies in the same market. This, in itself, is not unreasonable if
they are efficient competitors. It is the choice of demarcation line
between high and low market share that causes a brief operational
hiatus. Second, all classifications have to incorporate managerial-
specific perceptions that embrace a distilled knowledge of the
corporate 'whole' and the operational markets. Consequently, for
each corporate whole, the growth-share matrix is necessarily
different. It is often the result of several drafts, both internal and
external, to the company. The weighted whole should be the result
of combining managerial judgements with more objective macro-
data on market share and growth rate. Academic studies of the
Wind, Mahajan and Swire type have difficulty in incorporating the
former 'judgemental' elements and therefore, in the absence of a
thorough knowledge of the actual executive decisions, will always
yield disparate results.

Third, the demarcation lines are not arbitrary. It has been argued
that they incorporate accumulated experience, judgement and
sound 'macro' data. Wensley (1987) has rightly stated that there is a
presumption that the cell boundaries (i.e. demarcation line settings
at, say, 10 per cent growth or 1.5 per cent market share) represent some
'crucial discontinuity' along the axes. Points on either side of the
line should, theoretically, have more in common with others in their
cell and be somehow markedly different from others just on the
other side of the line. In many empirical cases, growth rates and
market shares follow continuously along their scales. There is no

'natural' demarcation or discontinuity in their incremental progression. In markets where discontinuities do exist, it is obvious where the lines should be drawn. But, more commonly, it is a matter of sound judgement in specific circumstances as to where they are placed along a continuous (not discontinuous) scale. There is rarely a quantum leap between one cell and another. It is usually a marginal progression.

Carelessly drawn demarcation lines lead to misclassifications of businesses. Consequently, the wrong strategic options can be suggested and even chosen. These misclassifications have become the source of much adverse criticism. But this is as much to do with poor analysis, judgement and lack of care in the construction and use of the matrix as the fault of the matrix itself. The real issue is whether the matrix facilitates an entry to strategic thinking for organizations as a first-phase or analytical tool. The acid test is whether strategic decisions are better with or without the tool. If the tool is a hammer, presumably, it helps knock nails in more efficiently than before hammers were invented. But it will not build the modern house on its own.

Practically, if the guidelines for cell boundaries are giving cause for concern regarding correct classification, managers should simply return to the original version of the box and erase the demarcation lines. Senior executive programme participants see this as a major breakthrough in viewing the whole corporate activities in a fresh way and avoiding the boxing in of strategic vision. Their secret is not to allow the tool to do anything more than it was designed for.

Framework

The potential for a square or rectangular four-cell matrix exists once the axes and guidelines are in position. However, there is a valid scientific principle that must, at least theoretically, be endorsed before the matrix is deemed to be 'logical'. The chosen dimensions (for the BCG matrix = growth and share) must be independent, rather than correlated, if the axes are to be perpendicular. A right-angle (90°) between the axes implies a zero correlation between the variables forming the adjoining axes. If the variables are correlated, the framework collapses gradually as the angle between them (denoting correlation) becomes more acute. The square or rectangle effectively becomes a diamond and, at the point where the dimensions are 100 per cent correlated, it reduces to a straight line.

Clearly, correlated variables cannot, theoretically, form square or rectangular boxes. For the BCG matrix, there is (in reality) a relationship between market growth and market share if the firm and its competitors are assumed to influence the dynamics of the market. The extent of the relationship will differ for each market. The expansion strategies of a monopolist, for instance, will have a more dramatic impact on market growth in a concentrated market than those of an atomistic firm in a fragmented market. Hence, it has to be assumed, especially as many of the active users of portfolio matrices are large players in their markets, that there is a degree of correlation between market growth and market share in reality. For all practical purposes this correlation has to be ignored in the construction of the matrix but it must be given detailed attention later when the strategy-formulation process concentrates on industry, market and organization dynamics in more detail.

Definition of business units

The area of the circles on the matrix is proportional to the total sales generated by a particular business. The definition of the business is crucial for the correct construction of the growth-share matrix. Organizations attempting to operationalize the matrix often face a dilemma between the theoretical optimum definition and the one recognized from developed practice. The optimum must comprise an economically distinct, independent and autonomous business grouping. If there is any link (e.g. transfer pricing) between the business units, the competitive strength, performance and strategic direction of each business cannot be singularly and clearly addressed. Hence, one of the underpinning reasons for the matrix collapses. Hax and Majluf (1984) consider this to be 'mandatory', lest business be misclassified giving: 'Dogs which are healthy, cash cows which have no milk, Question Marks which are not questionable and Stars which are not shining.'

In practice, most companies have a definition of a business group for reporting and other purposes. Data is generated along standard lines for these groups and is well understood by operational managers and at the centre. Any change towards a 'theoretical' optimum can create antagonism through suspicion and hence incur a resistance. Any new figure would also require a comprehensive overhaul of existing information systems and may, therefore, be expensive in cost (but probably not strategic) terms. Hence, many organizations (e.g. Black & Decker) stick to their existing group definitions when developing a matrix – an implicit recognition that, as this is a first phase of strategic thinking, notions of a theoretical optimum must yield to pragmatic initiatives. In doing this, managerial perceptions are rightly given a crucial and central role.

Other operational issues

Negative business growth

The matrix is sometimes criticized for its focus on markets with positive growth rates. To correct for negative rates requires a simple extension of the vertical axis downwards. Businesses can still generate positive net cash flows in declining markets by, for instance, retaining market share by buying up the capacity of their competitors who are leaving the market. Indeed, businesses previously classified as 'dogs' may increase market share in this way and become classified as cash cows in declining markets. Albeit the net positive cash flows are likely to have a finite life in these circumstances.

Dynamics

The matrix is often criticized for being static. It is like a balance sheet, providing a cross-sectional corporate portrait at one point in time. The operational solution is simply to form a regular series of matrices (e.g. quarterly) and to add directional arrows illustrating 'intent' and directional arrows illustrating previous positions. In this manner, it is easy to compare the actual and intended profiles in a budgetary variance-like fashion while adding a sense of time in the process.

Subjectivity

Perhaps the most frequently echoed operational criticism from both managers and MBA students is the subjectivity that is built into the matrix. 'It depends who is doing it.' It is possible for politically powerful line managers to force through a matrix display that shows their SBU in a strong and, hopefully, developing position. This may not appear to be so when the corporate whole is considered but, if the centre is weak, the political power could win through. The centre continues to make decisions in favour of the SBU, perpetuating the imbalance. Such an imbalance can also occur from strong functional specialists. There is always a difference in matrices constructed by accountants and those constructed by marketeers for the same organization given the same information. Moreover, any imbalance is exacerbated if the centre is strong and location-based. Many UK multinationals view themselves as global companies, even though their international portfolios are completely Anglo-Saxon in spread. This can colour their view of the potential of high-performing SBUs elsewhere.

Given there is a degree of subjectivity, the operational objective is to reduce it. There are two design elements that are helpful in avoiding or, at least, reducing the degree of subjectivity. First, within the company, mixed teams of functional, international and line/staff experiences are needed. Second, to avoid an overt internal focus, another membership cohort should include external appraisers such as consultants, analysts, customers and suppliers. The most successful portfolios are often constructed when a competitor is asked to state an honest opinion. Perspectives are remarkably different and can even be individually inconsistent over time.

The operational difficulties, overall, are relatively easy to accommodate. It is important that detailed attention is given to market measurement, to scales, to guidelines and to the definition of business units. Consideration should later be given to the dynamics of competition in the strategy-formulation process. But at this embryonic stage, the simple tool, if used carefully, is a powerful one for the task for which it was designed. As Howe (1986) says:

> Inevitably, the matrix is too simple to allow for every nuance of market conditions. No account is taken, for example, of the different risks attached to individual product interests, or, of the need to balance risks, as opposed to cash flows, in the product portfolio ... or sometimes a firm may be prepared to lose money in one product area if this leads to sales and profits in another. Or, more generally, a firm will carry a range of products as part of its sales policy without expecting to earn the same return on each line. It is difficult to see how the BCG matrix can be applied to these situations.

'It is difficult to see' because the matrix was never intended to view these things. It is the expectation that the hammer can saw wood and turn screws that is a false one. The hammer, none the less, can be judged efficient at knocking in nails.

Dangers

The dangers associated with the naive use of the growth-share matrix are plentiful. Most stem from a lack of awareness of the validity of key underlying assumptions as circumstances change for the organization.

Competition and market structure

There are two problems:

1   The matrix focuses on only one competitor for its relative market-share measure on the horizontal axis. That competitor is large. The danger of this upward competitive focus is to ignore fast-growing smaller firms who may pose the greater competitive threat in the medium term. The natural indication is then to look inward and ignore the competitive dynamics of the wider market place.

2   This relative measure only considers two players at most in a market. Consequently, the overall market structure – whether fragmented or concentrated, is not fully captured. Hence analysis of competitive dynamics is required in addition to the growth-share matrix. A starting point could be the framework proposed by Porter (1980; 1985) involving a close examination of the power of buyer and suppliers, the role of substitutes and barriers to entry in driving competitiveness. Moreover, users should be aware that the growth-share matrix is not good at dealing with monopolistic (one major seller) or perfectly competitive (many independent sellers) market structures. It is, however, more appropriate for intermediate structures e.g. oligopolies (few sellers) – which is the commonest market structure in the developed world.[12]

Value-added chain

The problem of measuring markets has already been discussed as a difficulty above. There is a danger that the market share actually measured is restricted to the end of the value added chain. This chain moves from R&D, through manufacturing, sub-assembly, marketing, distribution to retailing. The advantage of higher market share is reflected in accumulated experience that lowers cost. However, the impact of experience on direct costs at each of the value-added stages is different. The largest impact is likely to be in sub-assembly, then manufacturing, then distribution and marketing, and then R&D and retailing. Moreover, experience is likely to accumulate at different rates at each stage depending upon the product mixes and accumulated volumes passing through each. Experience may accrue more rapidly to those stages that are more heavily loaded by the complete set of items produced.

Measuring market share at the final stage of a value-added chain effectively ignores these two experience effects of differential impact and rate of accumulation. For example, company A could enjoy a 4:1 market-share advantage over company B at the manufacturing stage. But it would be erroneous to confirm its dominant position over B until other stages are taken into account. If B has superior access to distribution services with a 3:1 market-share advantage over A, then, taken together, the overall dominance in market share of A over B is much reduced. The competitive strengths of a firm cannot be measured by market share at the end of the value-added chain alone.

Time and change

Berle and Means (1932) were among the first researchers to identify that, by the 1930s, there was a divorce of ownership from control in large companies. Shareholders were so fragmented they held little sway over the ambitions of managers. Managers were able to pursue objectives other than profit maximization. They gained salary, prestige and status from growth. For a long period, while the divorce was effective, growth became the dominant corporate objective. During the late 1970s and throughout the 1980s in the UK, powerful institutional shareholders emerged, closely monitoring their corporate investments and so reducing the latitude of movement by executives. Growth was fashionable in the 1960s and 1970s when the growth-share matrix emerged. It can be argued that such growth rates are not now so freely pursued as a corporate objective by many organizations. Moreover, high market share is not the only route to profitability. Much research discussed in Chapter 4, has shown that companies with low shares in their markets can readily earn high relative returns with appropriate strategies (see later).

Oligopoly

Time has also witnessed a change in the manner of competition. Price-competition in perfectly competitive markets was, according to classical economic theory, the means by which these markets cleared. The joint-stock companies of the nineteenth century best reflected the atomistic behaviour of firms in such markets. But as firms have grown larger, the twentieth century has witnessed a movement towards other types of market structure, especially oligopoly (few, powerful sellers). This has been accompanied by a shift from price to non-price competition.

The basis for the experience curve is the falling off of costs as volume output expands. Henderson has acknowledged this in the examples at Norton and the General Instrument Company earlier. Where price competition is intense, it pays to be a low-cost producer, with the price-cost margin acting as a safety 'wedge'. Much of the development of learning curve and experience curves reflected price-competitive markets. Oligopolists, on the other hand, generally compete with non-price weaponry where the emphasis is on advertising, product quality and differentiation. Certainly, the importance of cost control is recognized, but, cost minimization recedes in importance when consideration is given to the additional cost of providing the market with a different product or service. Consequently, the horizontal axis of market share on the growth-share matrix and its underlying minimum cost, market-share gain proposition is called into question. High-volume output is necessarily restricted as companies pursue niche strategies (e.g. Rover, Volvo, Saab, in the automobile industry). The lack of growth in the European car industry in the early part of the 1990s, together with their lack of significant market share in the industry as a whole, would render all these 'nichers' to the dog category. Once again, the growth-share matrix needs to be reinforced and upgraded, especially if it is to be an effective tool in the 1990s.

Product/industry life cycle

These well known 'biological' cycles dictate the movement of businesses/products across the growth-share matrix. Question marks are at embryonic or early growth stages, stars are at later growth stages and cash cows are at the mature or decline stage. The natural movement along the cycle marks the ideal route for products. The other crucial movement, that of cash flow, necessitates the shifting of cash from cows to question marks and/or problem children. The source of cash (the cows) is dependent upon a long plateau stage of maturity in the life cycle to maintain the business's or product's dominant market position. As Slatter (1980) points out, this phase may be short lived and the whole policy of investing in question marks and stars from a fountain of funds in cash cows is misplaced. Industry or product evolution analysis is therefore an essential accompaniment to the initial growth-share analysis.

Strategic management

Nomenclature/political process

The selection of labels for each cell in the matrix is important. Dogs had originally been pets or, at the Mead Paper Corporation, mortgage businesses. Managers are seen to be losers if their business consistently features as a 'dog' (Haspeslagh 1982). This 'vulgar and destructive vocabulary' (Andrews 1981) can heavily influence resource allocation decisions in favour of the more attractive labels. Strategy formulation and implementation is, after all, far from being a value-free process. It is the outcome of organizational politics. The real risk, according to Morrison and Wensley (1991), is that:

the strategically crucial part of the exercise, the definitions of markets, SBUs and share, may be distorted by subsidiary managers for reasons of pride or self-interest, and that this may be undetectable to the 'distant' corporate executives.

The problem is likely to become acute if the subsidiary manager knows he is likely to be classified in the 'dog' cell.

Simplicity and precision

The simplicity and apparent precision of the growth-share matrix in classifying businesses can lead dangerously to the adoption of strategies for market situations which, although broadly similar, have distinct elements that require specific rather than generic strategy approaches. Harrigan and Porter (1983) in their research of 'end game' strategies in industries in long-term decline, found two other profitable strategies – leadership and niche – besides the generic, prescriptive one of divestment. On its own, the growth-share matrix cannot possibly be expected to reveal the conditions appropriate to each. Unfortunately, the perceived precision with which the matrix offers up the generic 'divestment' option can mislead the unwary or novice operator.

Most businesses in Europe tend to be smaller than their American or Japanese counterparts in terms of market share. As McNamee (1988) points out, in recessional situations most of them would be classified as dogs. It is easy to see the reasons why good businesses can be so classified and how, unfortunately, many of them must have succumbed to the divestment option selected by strategic decision makers at the centre.

All of these dangers, however, can be avoided with care and skill in construction and interpretation and building upon the growth-share matrix by adding supporting analytical frameworks to aid strategic choice.

Damaging criticisms

The operational difficulties associated with the growth-share matrix can be easily overcome. Safeguards can also be taken against inherent dangers in its use by bolstering the initial analysis with the use of other tools and techniques. There are, however, a third group of criticisms frequently aimed at the matrix. When charted against its original intended use they can be seen as largely irrelevant, misplaced and therefore as 'damaging'. They do, however, provide insights for further analyses.

Risk-return [13]

Howe (1986) noted earlier (p. 23) that the matrix gives no account of the risk attached to each product interest or of the need to balance risks as opposed to cash flow in the portfolio. Furthermore, the return on the individual 'automatic strategies' – like harvest, hold, grow and divest – is not shown. Clearly, it is impossible for this simple tool to do either of these in its basic form. It was never intended to be more than a first-phase analysis. The risk and return on individual projects has to be separately assessed using other techniques (e.g. NPV, DCF, payback).

The dependent variable moving across the cells in the growth-share matrix is cash flow. The above argument intimates that this should be replaced by returns. An enlightening attempt is provided by Hax and Majluf (1984). They present a 'theoretically better grounded approach for strategic investment planning', claiming that it represents a significant challenge to the conclusion derived from the growth-share matrix. It can be summarized in three statements:

1   There is a trade-off between profit and growth as corporate objectives. A business with a decreasing market-share strategy would be more selective in its investment projects leading to a higher return on investment (ROI) than a business following an increasing market-share strategy which would have to accept more marginal projects that would lower the ROI.

2   All profitable investment opportunities should be taken. Each one should be judged on its own merits and accepted or rejected depending on whether its projected return on investment falls above or below the cost of capital associated with that investment opportunity. There is no financial synergy; projects are additional.

3   Ideal business portfolios are not necessarily balanced in terms of internal cash flows. Zakon had described businesses as cash generators and cash users. A balanced portfolio in the BCG sense would have some businesses in each category. Some would be earning more than the firm's cost of capital, others less. Yet cash generation does not have to equate to high ROI. It is possible to have a portfolio consisting of all cash generators, each earning above the firm's cost of capital. IN BCG terms, this portfolio would be imbalanced, but in terms of returns it would be enviable in the short term.

This is a markedly different, though valuable, approach to the growth-share matrix. Its focus on returns rather than cash flow is an important change in emphasis, highlighting the additional trade-offs available to managers. In this sense, it should accompany rather than replace a BCG initiative.

In a related way, the dependent variable (cash flow) has drawn other criticism. Wensley (1981) has argued that there is a temptation to see the matrix as depicting a corporation that is an independent financial recycling entity, transferring funds from cash generators to cash users, ad infinitum. In this process, divestments have to occur to generate sufficient internal funding for growth. It appears that the capital market as an alternative source of funds is almost ignored. Yet Henderson's original paper (1970) talks about leverage and the stock market's role in controlling it, and so recognizes the connections between share price, gearing and returns. Morrison and

Wensley (1991) later acknowledge Henderson's recognition and admit that the original criticism may have been misplaced. The focus on internal fundings could however, readily be placed in the 'dangers' category above as a 'cautionary' tale, i.e. finance strategy should follow investment strategy and not constitute a predictor variable.

Strategic statements and implementation

The simple strategy statements offered by the matrix are an indication of where the firm should go. Critics have pointed out that the matrix does not provide any indication of how to get there (Lorenz 1981). How do you 'harvest' a cash cow? How do you operationalize the strategic decisions? Clearly it is not the intended purpose of the matrix to do this. The matrix can generate mission statements if used with 'care and discipline' but it is not a guide to strategy implementation. It is the starting point for analysis.

Focus

From early days (Abell and Hammond 1979) to the modern era (Hewitt 1988) critics have debated the narrowness of focus of the growth-share matrix. At bottom, it is accused of being just too simple. That corporate or business-unit strategy should be determined by one dependent (cash flow) and two (more or less) independent variables (growth and share) is just too optimistic an expectation. Hence, the critics claim, the matrix is not comprehensive enough. In the Warwick Survey (1989) 24 per cent of respondents rated the simplicity of the matrix as a key benefit while another 26 per cent rated it as a weakness. It is not just a matter of differing perceptions. The matrix is meant, like all good tools and models, to be simple. That is its real strength. Additional variables can be added to build other matrices (see below) and additional analyses can be conducted to support the original one. These are both discussed more fully below.

MATRIX EXTENSIONS

GE business screen

A proliferation of matrices followed the introduction of the growth-share matrix in the early 1970s. By 1981, 4 matrices were in common use and 5 others in circulation (Wind and Mahajan 1981). The American General Electric Company developed portfolio planning in parallel with BCG (Schoeffler *et al.* 1974). Theirs is probably the best known alternative, although, there are others that extend and improve the BCG matrix in a similar way (e.g. Shell's directional policy matrix).

The nine-cell business screen is shown in Figure 1.5. It adds to, and improves upon, BCGs growth-share matrix in several ways.

1   Market growth and market share are replaced as single indicators of industry attractiveness and competitive strength by composite parameters, constructed from factors selected and weighted by management, and relevant to each SBU. Sample factors and weightings are given in the accompanying notes to Figure 1.5 for industry attractiveness and competitive strengths, respectively.[14]

2   The area of the circle is proportional to the size of the industries in which the various businesses compete; the slices within them represent the market share of each business.

3   Axes are extended to give a wider positioning choice (3×3) and measurements are no longer in logarithms or percentages. Managerial judgement is the deciding factor for the location of businesses on the grid.

Hofer matrix

Critics argue that neither BCGs growth-share matrix nor the GE screen provide an indication of the position of new businesses that are just beginning to expand in new industries or markets. This is not a deserving criticism of the BCG matrix. On a simplified four-cell array, with axes of market growth and market share, it is quite impossible to show this evolutionary development with any degree of accuracy and without distorting the main purpose of the matrix. The solution is simple. BCGs matrix growth-share again forms the basis of a further extension and improvement. The fifteen-cell matrix, developed by Hofer (1977), depicted in Figure 1.6, shows competitive position plotted against the stages of product/market evolution. The circles and their wedges represent industry size and business market share as in the GE screen. However, the vertical axis shows the stage of product market evolution from development to decline. It is easy to identify growing businesses and hence, any imbalances in the 'cycle'.

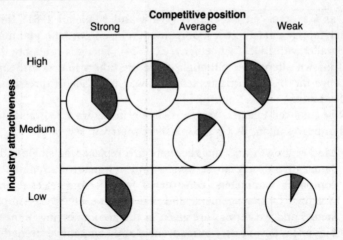

Figure 1.5 GE business screen

Notes: The vertical axis in the GE matrix is industry attractiveness, being an aggregate weighting of a parsimonious selection of the most important factors specific to any individual organization's industry. Each factor is given a weight according to its importance and then a rating on a 5 point scale (where 1 is very unattractive and 5 is very attractive) denoting how the organization performs against each. Weights are then multiplied by ratings giving values. This column is then aggregated to give the final score on the vertical axes. There is a temptation to consider this approach as scientific. Care must be taken to avoid subjectivity (see text).

eg.

Industry Attractiveness Factor	Weight	Rating	Value
Market size	0.20	4	0.80
Projected Market Growth	0.15	4	0.60
Profitability	0.20	3	0.60
Competitive structure	0.15	3	0.45
Cyclicality	0.10	2	0.20
Technology required etc.	—	—	

Weights should sum to 1.0.

A similar exercise is conducted for the horizontal axis – e.g.

Competitive Position Factor	Weight	Rating	Value
Market share	0.10	5	0.50
Distribution Net	0.20	4	0.80
Breadth of Product Line	0.05	4	0.20
Advertising Effectiveness	0.05	4	0.20
Experience Curve Effects	0.20	4	0.80
Relative Product Quality	0.15	4	0.60

Weights should sum to 1.0.

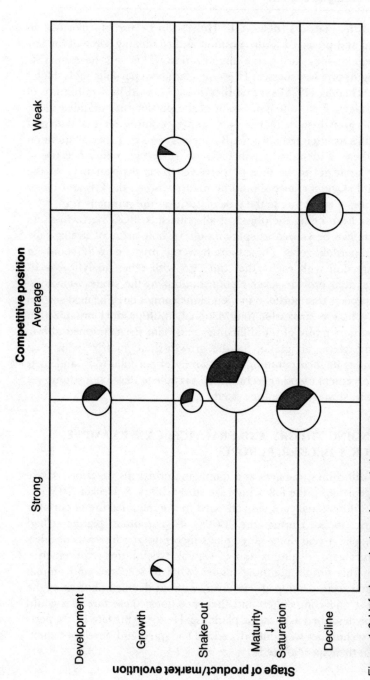

Figure 1.6 Hofer's product market evolution matrix
Source: Hofer and Schendel (1978)

All the matrices (BCG, GE, Hofer) can be used to plot out an actual and preferred future position and so identify some of the key strategic issues facing the organization. They all have specific strengths and weaknesses. They are a family of portfolio tools. Hofer and Schendel (1978) suggest they must be used in a minimum of two stages. First, a tentative plot of the portfolio is compiled using BCG's growth-share matrix. It is simple, requires the least data and so fulfils its intended purpose. Businesses requiring special attention can then be identified for inclusion in stage two, either because of their strategic importance or perceived poor performance. At the second stage, a choice should be made between the GE and Hofer matrices – according to the type of business the company is in.

Far from being the object of all criticisms, BCG's growth-share matrix can be viewed as sparking off a whole array of strategically useful portfolio tools. These tools, however, must be used not only in conjunction with each other but also with other analytical techniques that provide specific contributions to the strategy-formulation process that portfolio models alone cannot do. The next section shows how a successful multinational, multiproduct organization encounters many of the difficulties and dangers mentioned above. By the clever adaptation of the growth-share matrix to its own business, its incorporation into a family of portfolio tools and their reinforcement by other techniques, it is able to develop a strong, yet flexible, strategic-planning system.

BLENDING THEORY AND PRACTICE: CASE EXAMPLE, BLACK & DECKER, EUROPE[15]

The difficulties, dangers and damaging criticisms described above are depicted in the following case study. Black & Decker (BD) is a US multinational company engaged in the manufacture of portable electric tools. During the 1970s, its corporate planners had developed 4-year, long-range plans incorporating forecasts of sales, product gaps, of profits and of capital expenditure requirements. From this simple planning model 'what if' scenarios and annual budgets were developed. However, without detailed analysis of the market and competitors and their reactions, these forecasts could not be described as strategic planning. Hence in the late 1970s, portfolio techniques were introduced. BD adapted and developed them to suit their specific needs.

Politics

When considering the practical application of portfolio management for Black & Decker Europe, it was of paramount importance to remember at all times that the business was run by the management of the company and not by a technique or series of charts.

(Walker 1990)

This is an important statement. In the introductory stage, it was necessary to gain the acceptance, understanding and commitment of operating managers and involve them in the planning process. BD initially used portfolio analysis to stimulate strategic thought within the top management group. But they quickly moved to incorporate it into a broader planning framework, embracing the inputs of operational managers from the earliest days. In doing this, they overcame many of management's objections to portfolio analysis and avoided theoretical pitfalls. They did however face a series of difficulties and dangers.

Difficulties and dangers

1 *Definition of business units*:
   • each needed unique market characteristics;
   • management had to agree on definitions;
   • data had to be readily available.
2 *Validity of the data*: data didn't have to be '100 per cent accountancy accurate' but consistent and recognizable by operating managers. Trends rather than details were assessed.
3 *Intended response*: the growth-share matrix alone did not (and cannot) show BD's intended response in terms of sales, returns and profitability.
4 *Market structure*: the growth-share matrix only considered one competitor and gave no indication of market structure.

Simple form

The original growth-share matrix was used as a first-phase approach. BD adopted the simple form (see Figure 1.7) to suit their circumstances.

• The market-share breakpoint was given as 1½ times that of the

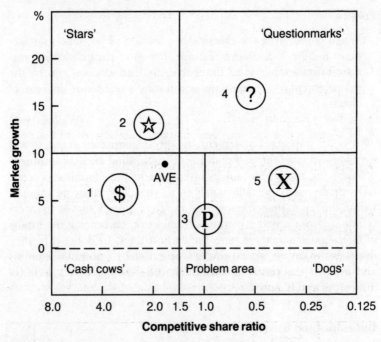

Figure 1.7 Simple form of the growth-share matrix
Source: Walker (1990)

nearest large competitor, although they left the original line on
the grid at 1.0 for comparative purposes.
- The market-growth breakpoint reflected the company's overall
  growth objective (10 per cent).

BD felt strongly that market structure (concentrated vs fragmented),
competitor reaction and market sizes of the businesses needed to be
plotted 'additionally' to support the strategic display of the simple
form. Hence data was gathered on all major competitors and on the
total market for all business units. It was important that operational
managers 'felt' happy that there was 'detail' beneath the display and
so decisions could be taken with some confidence.

Development

To support the growth-share matrix BD added a full competitor
analysis and further data describing sales, growth, profitability

growth and returns. These charts were designed to be viewed as a set or 'family of portfolios'.

Competitor analysis

This chart (see Figure 1.8) contains:

- Market size and growth rates.
- Competitor shares in each market, showing dominance (1) concentration (3) and fragmentation (4,5).
- Specialist competitors (e.g. F in product 2).
- Potential threats (e.g. C and E don't compete in any market so a merger/takeover of one by the other would be a major threat).
- Market leadership (A and notably E wherever it competes).
- Growth-share matrix ratio.

By superimposing these bar charts, period by period, BD have a dynamic view of changing market shares allowing them to plot the historical trends and forecast the evolution of the market environ-

Business	Market		Competitor shares							Ratio	Ref.
	Size	Growth									
Total	3500	8.5	A28	B14	C12	D10	E8	F4	O24	2.0	B
1	1000	5.0	A45	B8	C15	D11			O21	3.0	C
5	1000	7.5	A10	B30	C17	D15			O28	0.33	B
2	750	12.5	A36	B11	C13	F18			O22	2.0	F
4	500	15.0	A16	B8	D18	E32			O26	0.5	E
3	250	2.5	A40	E40					O20	1.0	E

Figure 1.8 Market and competitor analysis
Source: Walker (1990)

ment. This analysis was supported by a great deal of qualitative information on the activities of major competitors in businesses other than portable electric tools (e.g. Bosch and AEG had much wider interests) that BD took into account in examining their respective strengths and weaknesses.

Sales growth/share gain

This chart (see Figure 1.9) allows operational managers a chance to show their projected strategies, in terms of sales growth, once their actual position is established on the growth-share matrix at the first phase. If they are behind growth targets they have a choice of strategies: (1) take share; (2) extend into new markets; or (3) stimulate existing markets. The diagonal line separates off those businesses planning to lose share (above) and those planning to take share

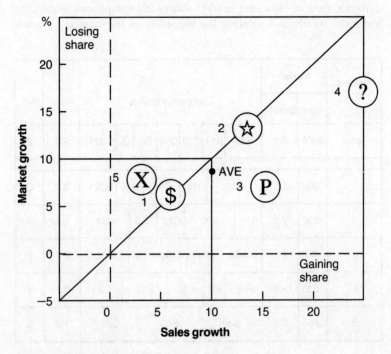

Figure 1.9 Sales-growth/share-gain chart
Source: Walker (1990)

(below) and the vertical and horizontal guidelines are BD's growth targets. Products 1 and 2 plan to maintain share, 3 and 4 to take share and 5 to be run down. Operational managers in charge of 3 are intent on influencing market growth as their forecast growth is higher than on the simple matrix. The circles represent contributions at the *end* of the period. Additionally, the chart recognizes that some products may compete in declining markets and provide for negative-growth projections below the zero-based horizontal axis.

Profitability analysis

In order to consider financial implications, BD developed two further charts (Figures 1.10 and 1.11) based upon a readily recognizable internal reporting measure – income before tax to sales. Figure 1.10 is deliberately constructed to be directly comparable to

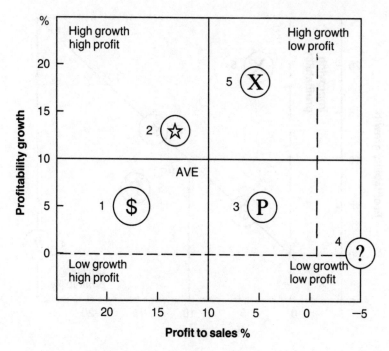

Figure 1.10 Profitability analysis chart
Source: Walker (1990)

the growth-share matrix. Most businesses fall out as expected e.g. high market share and high profitability (1) with those in low growth markets having low profit growth (3). But this is not always the case (e.g. 5,4). Hence, attention is focused on theoretical misfits and on profit planning in non-dominant businesses (3,4,5). Circles are current profit contributions and so can be compared directly with sales circles on the growth-share matrix.

Profitability growth/changes

Figure 1.11 is the parallel of sales growth/share gain chart with the horizontal axis from the latter transplanted to the former. The diagonal separates off increasing (above) from decreasing (below) profitability businesses. The circles are now projected profit contributions. In businesses 1 and 2 profit is maintained, 5 shows a rapid

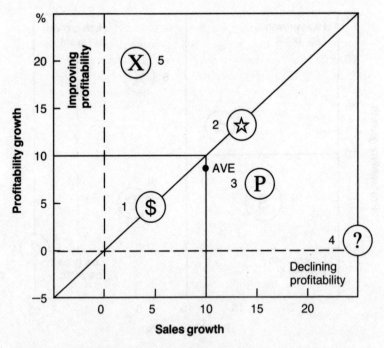

Figure 1.11 Profitability growth-change chart
Source: Walker (1990)

improvement due to short-run harvesting while 3 declines to fund a total change in the market and 4 declines to fund improvements in share. The latter two charts enable BD to map out share gain in profitability terms and identify problem areas in strategic response.

THE COMPLETE PLANNING CHART SET

The four charts (Figures 1.7, 1.9, 1.10 and 1.11) are a benchmark for operational managers. Specific strategies for each business are suggested:

1 *Cash cow*: maintain share and above average profit.
2 *Star*: must protect share even at expense of profit.
3 *Problem*: new market change strategies will be expensive, thus reducing profits.
4 *Question mark*: increases in share needed, losses accepted if it means growth.
5 *Dog*: harvested and divested.

Note that only after rigorous analysis at BD, are these strategies suggested for dogs. They are not automatic prescriptions. Overall, the charts show, that BD needs to gain share in its markets to achieve its 10 per cent objective, yet their gains will be paid for by reduced profitability, although this will remain above average (see Figure 1.12).

The lessons

The major factors for successful implementation at BD were that:

• Techniques and displays must be simple and relevant.
• Information must be easily recognizable to managers.
• Management must manage the company, not consultants nor theories.

Vesper (1983) commented that 'matrix displays are an impressive tool but nothing more, they can be used as a "first" orientation but real strategic planning only begins at this point'. This view is one clearly and profoundly shared by BD in the implementation of their planning system.

The Black & Decker case study emphasizes the first-phase use of the growth-share matrix and its adaption and development to local business conditions. It helps start strategic thinking but falls short of prescribing remedies on its own.

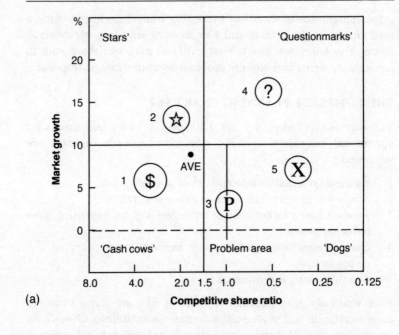

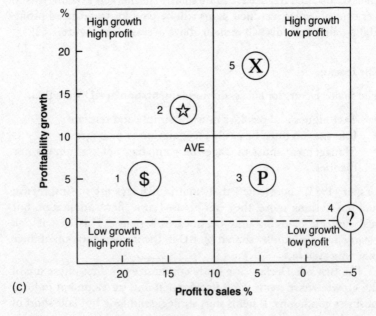

Figure 1.12 The planning chart set

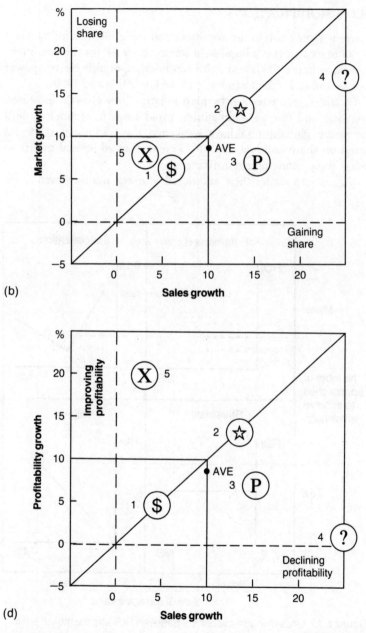

(b)

(d)

Source: Walker (1990)

BCG'S MODIFICATIONS

There is some truth in the argument that the growth-share matrix is a tool of its age. It is a hand-held hammer, useful for the conditions prevailing in the 1960s and 1970s but not the portable electric power tool necessary for the turbulence of the late 1970s and 1980s.

Changes, characterized by high inflation, low growth, increased domestic and foreign competition, rapid leaps in technology and increasing globalization have weakened the traditional strategies based on share and low cost. BCG created an additional matrix to reflect these changing circumstances.

Figure 1.13 shows their additional four-cell matrix based upon

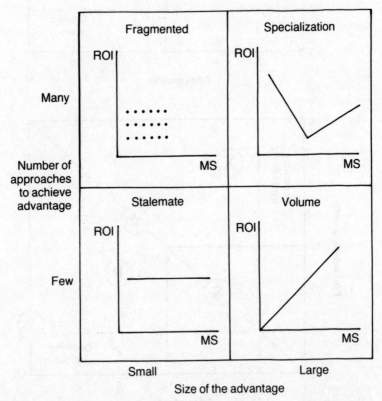

Figure 1.13 Underlying relationships between ROI and market share in the new BCG matrix

Source: Adapted from Hax and Majluf (1984)

size of competitive advantage and number of ways in which the advantage can be achieved. It also illustrates the underlying relationships for each, designated by an ROI-market share mapping.

Volume depends upon the share/low-cost strategy associated with the original growth/share matrix (e.g. General Motors, Toyota, Ford as global players in the automobile industry).

Stalemate businesses operate in industries where profitabilities are low for all firms irrespective of size. *Fragmented* businesses operate where profitability is not linked to market share. There are many ways of achieving an advantage for both small and large firms, success depends upon who exploits them best.

The *Specialization* cell indicates a disjointed relationship between profitability and market share. Smaller businesses have a higher profitability level through the pursuance of focus strategies (e.g. Honda[16] in breaking into the US automobile market).

The additional matrix is not a replacement for the original form, which, as has been shown, still has a very effective role to play in the initial stimulus of strategic thinking. But it does provide a better insight into market structural conditions, in the dynamics of competition and in the suggestion of a wider variety of generic strategy options. Hax and Majluf (1984; 1991) observe that the only way a firm can defend a long-term advantage is through entry barriers which, therefore, must underpin the horizontal axis of the additional matrix. The vertical axis must be linked to differentiation from wide to narrow focus. The link with Porter's (1980; 1985) generic strategies of cost leadership (volume), differentiation (fragmentation) and focus (specialization) is evident. Porter's (Harvard Business School, Boston) framework is a development and repackaging of much of the 1960s and 1970s industrial organization orthodoxy stemming from Bain's (Harvard) research in the 1950s. The academic output at Harvard and the pragmatic work of the Boston Consulting Group are closely intertwined; together they possess a powerful marketing machine that has facilitated the widespread adoption of their techniques so that they came to be regarded, by many, as the strategy orthodoxy of the 1970s (BCG matrix) and 1980s (Porter's five forces).

As a cautionary note, these approaches are strongly location bound in their underpinning research (US/UK manufacturing industry). The accumulation of quality data is necessary for its successful operation. Hence, the orthodoxy can fall down where information is tight or restricted (e.g. on private companies in Spain and Germany, China, most African nations, Eastern Europe, India and Russia, i.e. where most of the future growth is likely to be). Moreover, this work is heavily rooted in the paradigms of the 'old' industrial organization school. It would be interesting to conjecture if the new industrialization school or the 'contestable market' school (Baumol, Panzer and Willig 1982), given Harvard's and BCGs marketing resources, were able to push more competitive tools onto the strategic scene for the 1990s.

The additional matrix copes with both price (volume) and non-price (fragmented, specialization) competition. In addition, it is necessarily more comprehensive with the penalties of cost and ease of communication to operating managers that this extra detail entails. Hence, there is still a central role for simplicity. For the 1990s, the BCG is heavily involved in its consultancies with the notion of 'time-based' competition in markets. Time and tools move on, but sometimes the simple ones are still the best.

CONCLUSIONS

There are operational 'difficulties' and inherent 'dangers' for the unwary in the construction and use of the original BCG matrix. However, as has been shown, most of these can be overcome or avoided by careful implementation and sensible use of support portfolios and other analytical tools. There are, of course, a host of 'damaging' criticisms that are misplaced. However, in themselves, they offer other insights to analytical content and form, in adaptation and development that are essential for best practice in strategy formulation.

The original matrix is still an impressive tool in its simplicity, wide understanding and appeal. It shifts the focus of attention away from internal profit centres and rightly concentrates on markets (and their definitions), growth, profit, sales, competitive threats and reactions and cost competitiveness through experience curve effects. Managers at the Mead Paper Corporation regarded the shift from profit centres to markets as *the* most important contribution of the matrix. This shift forces managers to change their perspectives in consideration of longer-term priorities (Haspeslagh 1982). Moreover, its effective use rests on the support and commitment of operational managers and involves them in the political process of strategy making. As seen in the Black & Decker case, the matrix can be adapted and customized for individual organizations which, once more, underlines the ownership of the tool by managers who manage.

But its greatest virtue lies in its simplicity. It was originally intended to be a presentational device and so as a starting point for strategic thinking. Even in the 1990s, its simplicity and clarity in serving this purpose cannot be questioned. It has no peers as a tool. Changing environmental circumstances may have marginally limited its use and effectiveness but this need not suffer if other techniques are constructed to support it. Moreover, critics argue that it has been contained within orthodox management teaching and practice for so long that it can no longer confess to have a competitive advantage. In well developed, systematic strategic planning systems (mainly the large organizations), there is some truth in this 'cancellation' argument. There are two points. First, in strategy formulation, it matters not so much about tools and techniques in a planning system but about good strategies in the search for a competitive advantage. Obtaining good strategies involves the sensible use of effective tools and techniques. The growth-share matrix is one that it may be dangerous to eject from the analytical tool box. Second, there are thousands of organizations that have no systematic strategy process. Based upon the assumption that some systematic strategy formulation and implementation is more profitable than none at all, it makes sense for these organizations to adopt more formal practices. The easiest way to introduce and stimulate strategic thinking in these organizations is to use a simple tool like the growth-share matrix. Its simplicity facilitates the transfer of ownership from consultants/academics to operational managers – the key to successful implementation. In so doing, the matrix begins a new round of management education and 'roots' strategic thinking in the organization for the first time. Moreover, it still has a lasting value in organizations where the strategy process is well developed. Often this is not fully communicated to operational managers. If it is, it rarely travels very far down the line. Managerial motivation and commitment below SBU board level is critical to the effective achievement of strategic objectives. In post-experience executive programmes, the ease with which corporate strategies can be communicated to managers through this simple tool validates its continued existence. If a two-way dialogue is then generated between centre and operating unit, the utility of the tool is proven.

Great concern does, however, stem from the simplicity of the matrix. Sometimes organizations do not successfully overcome the operational difficulties or, more frequently, fall into the dangerous pitfalls associated with its naive use.

It is a real worry that the original matrix is so seductively simple, and the temptations and risks of using it 'off the shelf' are real. If the market is simply taken on the trade association figures, the competition as trade association members, the cost savings as materialising automatically from experiences, and (probably worst of all) the SBU as the existing operating unit (thereby fore-stalling possible discussion of restructuring), the use of the tech-nique would be at best unhelpful and at worst positively damaging. Those who now use it may be 'boxed in' in terms of restrictive assumptions about the nature of the market and competitive dynamics.

(Morrison and Wensley 1991)

The founding fathers are equally sceptical:

The matrix made a major contribution to strategic thought ... today it is misused and over exposed. It can be a helpful tool, but it can also be misleading, or worse, a straightjacket.

(Zakon 1981)

The growth share matrix was a milestone in the search for insights into business system dynamics, but certainly not the end of the road. We are far from using what we know to put it together in a fashion that permits us to be truly insightful about business system dynamics.

(Henderson 1988)

To help avoid the myopia attached to naive use and the consequent pitfalls, the investigation now turns to an exploration of the forgotten cell – the vulgar and destructively labelled dog. In particular, it is of concern that the generic strategy suggestion of divestment may be a serious form of 'boxing in'. The next chapter examines the debates on corporate recovery, especially from a mature or maturing base-line. How do previously stagnating businesses revive their performance?

Chapter 2

Corporate recovery

INTRODUCTION

In the first chapter, it was argued that one of the most influential strategy foundation tools of the 1970s and 1980s has been overstretched in operational usage. It had been forced into exercises for which it was not designed. Consequently, many business units containing good performance potential could have been erroneously classified as dogs and subjected to the automatic prescription of divestment. Many of these have been bought out by their management and, subsequently, enjoyed prosperous times. This chapter focuses upon corporate recovery – the rejuvenation of assets that may have been misclassified. The underlying theories are presented alongside the empirical research results. These are followed by a section for the practising manager on techniques of 'how to'. Clearly the main principles of recovery apply to all organizations, not solely to businesses within a larger portfolio. But it is with the latter in mind that the main tenor of the argument laid down in this chapter continues.

DIVESTMENT

When business units are placed in the dog category, the automatic prescription from the growth-share matrix is divestment. Unfortunately, in Europe during recessional periods, it is estimated that up to 80 per cent of businesses can be so described (McNamee 1988).

Divestment is an important strategy for organizations in a competitive environment. In its variety of forms – liquidation, buy-outs, buy-ins and de-mergers – it became increasingly popular during the 1980s. Howe has estimated that the proportion of divestments (as measured by the number of subsidiaries sold) to acquisitions rose from an average of 24 to 29 per cent from the early/mid-1970s to the early/mid-1980s in the UK. The annual figures fluctuate, but the adjusted average is certainly rising. Moreover, the rise in the average value of divestments as a proportion of acquisitions over the same period has been greater – from 14 to 23 per cent. Although this increase in number and value of divestments was accompanied by the increasing use of the growth-share matrix in strategy formulation by organizations, it is difficult and probably impossible to make a direct causal link.

The growth-share suggestion of divestment may be a credible one if it shifts resources away from declining traditional activities to higher growth and profitable markets, effectively repositioning the organization. This is a positive form of portfolio management. There are, however, many other sound reasons for divestment not directly related to portfolio management. First, acquisitions of whole organizations often end up with some unwanted businesses that do not have a direct strategic 'fit'. Their sale can be used to offset the cost of the total acquisition. Second, organizations may underestimate the resources (technical, financial or managerial) required to gain a competitive advantage in product markets which they have entered. Perhaps their entry was on the back of a fashionable trend such as energy efficiency. The number of companies seeking to enter the 'alternative-energy' market after oil-price rises in the 1970s and 1980s was considerable, both in the UK and US. Unfortunately the intensity of R&D in, for example, the generation of power from wave energy can sap the deepest of corporate purses. A strategic divestment and a reallocation of resources in this instance is an appropriate decision.

Finally, the performance of subsidiaries in certain sectors may be repeatedly unsatisfactory despite the constant application of efficiency measures and other remedies. Acquisition strategies may not have taken a full account of market demand and supply (especially cost) projections nor of the competitor reaction to the acquisition. Furthermore, insufficient pre-acquisition attention given to the soft (human, cultural) and hard (information technology, information systems) features of the two organizations may result in much lower returns than anticipated. For whatever reason, a de-merger of the acquired unit may be the only sensible option.

Besides these more positive reasons, there are a host of negative reasons for divestment tied to strategic failure, e.g. a high price paid

*of Charkham
1994
n Takeover r (see other
Acq'n re the other story.

for acquisitions, uncritical diversification policies, manageability of vast unrelated conglomerate organizations and 'survival through sale'. The problem is that divestment is often seen as an explanation of failure, as a judgemental error or as managerial incompetence. Hence, divestments can be highly charged with emotion, since much managerial pride (and future) is tied up in what becomes a psychological, rather than a strategic, decision. As Howe (1986) argues: 'So long as divestment is viewed as a negative strategy, then the decision to divest is likely to be left until it is too late to be effective.' Delay caused by emotional ties reduces the possibility of maximizing the gain from sale and limits the amount of re-positioning that is subsequently made possible by the release of resources. Hence, there are many arguments for divestment other than for direct portfolio management. The importance being, that if divestment is a credible option, it must be seen as a positive strategic decision in order to be efficient.

Despite these reasons, divestment should not be seen as an automatic, growth-share engineered prescription. As Zakon said, the growth-share matrix can become a straitjacket, resulting in instant strategy and by-passing or hindering quality strategic thought. Divestment may, after all, not be the only option on offer. Others may include strategies for recovery/rejuvenation, maturity, end game and internationalization. These may be credible alternatives for organizations, depending on the conditions in their task and general environments and on their internal strengths and weaknesses. The next section deals with corporate recovery.

EXPANDING LITERATURE BASE

The 1980s witnessed a re-balancing in the managerial literature in the attention it paid to the phenomenon of corporate recovery. In the mid 1970s, Argenti (1976) had suggested that probably 10 per cent (or 50,000) of all registered UK companies were in a state of failure. Bibeault (1982) estimated that 80 per cent or more of the 4,000 US Standard and Poor companies (representing 70 per cent of US corporate assets) had experienced severe earnings decline followed by a recovery. The managerial literature, at this time, paid scant attention to the issue. There was a lot of accountancy/consultancy-based material on failure and its prediction (see, for instance, Altman 1968) but little in terms of systematic analysis. Since the mid-1970s and especially during the 1980s, the position has ben rectified.

An article by Hoffman (1989) was much needed to summarize the host of empirically driven research studies during this time.

The literature can be separated into two parts: First, the academic-based studies that focus on the processes underlying decline and recovery and incorporate empirical testing of hypotheses; second, the pragmatically driven studies focusing on 'how to' prescriptions, based, somewhat shakily, on the assumption that all organizations and their situations are homogeneous. Later, we will examine the salient points from the latter literature. The academic counterweight provides a stronger understanding of the underlying process involved. This is a necessary step, as it allows the prescription for recovery to be more finely tuned to prevailing circumstances and hence to maximize the effectiveness of the recovery process.

CLASSIFICATIONS OF CORPORATE RECOVERY

Classification systems

The academic literature on corporate decline and the related literature on corporate crises is now well established (see Whetton 1987; Cameron, Sutton and Whetton 1988). In addition, contingency theory has triggered a significant number of classification systems in the strategic management/business policy literature.[1] These systems seek to categorize policies and strategies into discrete compartments based upon common characteristics. For example, Miles and Snow (1978) in one of the first and most significant attempts, split companies into prospectors, analysers, defenders and reactors, based upon characteristics associated with their strategies. Porter's lowest-cost producers and differentiators (focus or broad) is a similar classification attempt. These systems have great merit in enabling differentiation, generalization, identification and information retrieval. They are influential in the evolution of our knowledge by facilitating the theory–development–theory testing cycle. Unfortunately, many of them, including the most popular ones, (Porter 1980; 1985) have been criticized for problems such as omission of variables and measurement error (see Chrisman, Hofer and Boulton 1988). Hence, their general applicability is in some doubt. Because corporate situations can be so unique, the task of building useful, testable classification systems for business policy/strategy is a daunting one.

None the less, the issue of classification has had significant attention in one corner of the decline and crises literature – that pertaining to corporate turnarounds. Here, the systems distinguish between strategic and operating taxa (e.g. Schendel, Patten and Riggs 1976; Hofer 1980). The difference is between 'doing different things' and 'doing things differently'. In the former case, companies are involved in attempts to change their product-market stance by adjusting strategy, e.g. through acquisition or divestment. The latter case involves a fundamental change in the nature of the firm's operations to improve efficiency e.g. through the use of advanced manufacturing technology.

The distinction between strategic and operating turnarounds has been challenged by Hambrick and Schecter (1983). They argue that the difference between them becomes blurred as the unit of analysis shifts from the corporate to the business level. In turn, they have offered three primary turnaround categories. They have two small clusters in their sample of turnaround companies reflecting the more traditional asset-cost surgery and the less frequent one of product-market pruning. Their third, and largest, category represents piecemeal turnaround strategies. This dominant cluster would seem to suggest that turnaround strategies differ significantly enough between businesses that it is impossible to define a single turnaround gestalt. Hence, it is difficult to generalize properly about corporate turnaround strategies as individual corporate circumstances are unique.

A similar problem of adequate distinction occurs in the research on the sharp recovery of stagnating companies (see Grinyer, Mayes and McKiernan 1988). The basis for this sample are organizations that have achieved a sharp (less than 2 years) and sustained (greater than 5 years) recovery from a period of relative[2] decline (at least 5 years) in their industry. The UK sample of manufacturing companies is sufficiently broad across sectors, size and states of the decline to enable a detailed examination of the types of recovery employed by its organizations and how these are related to contextual variables. It provides the foundation for an empirically based classification system, by comparing the turnaround situation with other recoveries at different stages of corporate decline. Turnaround is only one type of corporate recovery. By broadening the category to incorporate other recovery situations, more meaningful and consistent recovery strategies can be identified.

Moreover, turnaround normally implies that companies are facing a financial situation of such gravity that something has to be done as a matter of urgency. This threat of extinction (the triggering force) may give rise to a series of actions – either strategic or operational, that are specific to circumstances at the time. Hence, they appear to researchers as large clusters of piecemeal strategies (see p. 53). By comparing turnaround with other recovery situations, the picture becomes clearer as the impact of other variables is examined, e.g. other motivational forces (the threat of takeover) other than a threat of extinction. Organizations that recover from positions of stagnation or decline without the immediate threat of extinction can manage this substantial change sharply (Grinyer, Mayes and McKiernan 1988) or gradually³ (Stopford and Baden-Fuller 1990).

The results of the above research studies allow us to piece together the process of corporate recovery in a generalizable format. A first step is to examine the decline stage by focusing upon how decisions are made generally within organizations. This requires a visit to the macro-organizational behaviour literature.

A MODEL OF ORGANIZATIONAL DECISION MAKING⁴

Much of the literature on organizational decison making and adaptation stems from the classic work of Cyert and March (1963). Their analysis is of bureaucratic, tradition-based, incremental decision making. This is characterized by a limited, simple search in response to problems; uncertainty avoidance by disregarding unpredictable future impacts; concentration on short-term feedback and negotiated environments; the quasi-resolution of conflict by sequential attention to goals and local rationality; and '*the use of standard operating procedures and rules*' for making decisions.

Such organizations adapt in two ways. First, through changes in their 'aspiration' levels. These are critical values of organizational goals determined as a function of past goals, previous experience regarding goals, and the goal performance of comparable organizations (latter day benchmarking). Second, they adapt through the evolvement of best-practice rules given the organization's past experience of success and failure. Organizations focus on operational decisions with short-run adaptation. They 'devote little time to long run planning ... and rely heavily on traditional methods, general industrial practice, and standard operating procedures for making decisions' (Cyert and March 1963: 100).

These slow, recursive, procedural responses to stimuli are well suited to the 'machine bureaucracies' that operate in mature markets with stable environments (see Mintzberg 1983; Burns and Stalker 1961). The problems arise when they face turbulence in their environments from, say, rapidly changing technology. Their historically determined structuration and distributions of power impede the major changes that are necessary in decline or crisis situations. Their major decisions are bound by habits, procedures and unreflective practices (Clark and Starkey 1988). They are reinforced by constant usage (even when no longer appropriate) and by corporate ideologies, sagas and myths (Clark 1979). These structural repertoires can understandably impede fundamental change. They represent years of investment in distilled knowledge and skills, in trading partners, in physical operations and geographic locations and in operational systems. Any change in one aspect of this corporate bundle involves writing off a substantial human and capital investment. Hence, change is going to be resisted.

The original Cyert and March model has been extended in the literature in three helpful ways:

1 The impediments to change in the Cyert and March model represented by conventional practices and standard operating rules are reinforced by the addition of operationally related sets of beliefs. These belief systems can shape environmental monitoring, responses to signals, aspiration levels of goals, and the search for, and selection from, appropriate strategic options. It is difficult to measure these cultural beliefs of 'how to do business' partly because they are rarely articulated, but they exist in all organizations, regardless of size. Pondy (1984) refers to them accurately as 'templates'.

2 The literature sees the co-existence of the two – the Cyert and March standard operating practices and the related belief systems, values and culture – as forming an almost impenetrable resistance to major change. In the short run, organizations adapt by first delegating responses to problems to functional areas where incremental operating solutions are found. If solutions are not forthcoming, a wider search process follows, leading to cost cutting in politically vulnerable areas such as overhead expenses or staff positions. The organization, unable to give up its structured practices and beliefs, is seen as eventually a short-term, operational, adaptive mechanism wherein difficulties must rise to crisis proportions before a fundamental change in its pattern of activities occurs.[5] Such crises frequently result in changes in leadership (either in a single leader or

collective leadership at the top), introducing a new dominant coalition with a new set of beliefs about 'how business should be done'. The actions taken by the dominant coalition leading change will be appropriate to the crisis context. However, it has recently been argued (see Pettigrew and Whipp 1991) that different business situations need different leadership styles and that, after the crisis is resolved and performance improves, a further change in leadership is necessary to sustain the improvement in corporate performance into the medium term. This would involve the replacement of a more autocratic leader (for the turnaround) by a more democratic leader (for the consolidation phase).

(3) The Cyert and March model has nothing to say about how organizations can adapt using 'higher level learning rules'. There are a number of facilitators that can help the machine bureaucracy to adapt more readily to broader strategic problems.

- Spender (1979) introduced the idea of a 'recipe' that reflects the 'best practice' manner of 'doing business' in any industry. The recipe is evolved by a small number of firms who, as a direct consequence, lead the industry. Their way of 'doing business' becomes widely imitated in the industry once its success is proven. Spender sees an internal cohesion within this industry recipe that reflects the best way of operating and so its adoption by other organizations ought to resolve internal corporate conflict on how to adapt. Changes in technology and markets may well dilute the importance of recipes over time but new ones will take their place as companies find the best way of operating. However, as Grinyer and Spender (1979) found, the introduction of a new recipe into a specific firm is likely to be resisted to the point at which a major crisis occurs and new top management with knowledge of it are put in place.
- Systematic, rational models of corporate planning (e.g. Ansoff 1968; 1984; Hax and Majluf 1984) and the bureaucratic processes in which they are embedded (e.g. Lorange and Vancil 1977) are intended to aid major strategic re-orientations in organizations, e.g. divestments, strategic alliances. Moreover, contingency theorists (Lawrence and Lorsch 1967) argue that consciously chosen organizational designs can promote more rapid response to the stimuli of complex environments.

Hence, the original Cyert and March model can be extended with a sequential search process directed by these higher-level learning rules. The search for solutions to problems can start with the Cyert and March focus on local operating issues and, failing a solution, employ a wider search procedure moving on through the 'politically vulnerable' to take in the entire corporate organization.

Such planning rules could indicate the appropriate level of response to problems. These can then be routed more directly to the operating, administrative or strategic decision taking units for a solution.[6] Grinyer (1971) and Grinyer and McKiernan (1990) have argued that this widening search process accords with the natural inclinations of the organization, as staying within its pattern of operations, rules and beliefs as long as possible. This reduces risk by restricting exposure to activities which the organization does not fully understand and with respect to which, it has no distinctive skills on which it may earn economic rent.

In this extended Cyert and March model, organizations respond to problems by utilizing a successive wider search process and stick with their standard operating patterns, beliefs and rules (OBRs) as long as the situation will allow. These OBRs are, however, a serious impediment to the major fundamental changes that are needed in times of severe crises, e.g. financial exigency. The extended model is presented diagrammatically in Figure 2.1. The sequential nature of the procedure can be seen as the organization widens its search for a solution through stages 1, 2 and 3. There are two features that now require emphasis – breaking the mould and learning through systematic planning.

Breaking the mould

At the heart of the model is the relationship between aspiration levels (internal and external, however measured) and actual organizational performance. Performance which fails to meet aspiration levels will, initially, stimulate a local search for marginal, incremental solutions, followed by tight control and cost cutting in politically vulnerable areas. Success in these areas leads, by short-term feedback, to some local adaptation of the standard operating rules and to their reinforcement. However, if this stage fails, the search for solutions widens to more strategic changes which involve changes in the disposition of resources, in the range of products, and in the markets served.

At this juncture, changes made do not involve jettisoning the existing operating policies, belief systems, rules, values and general

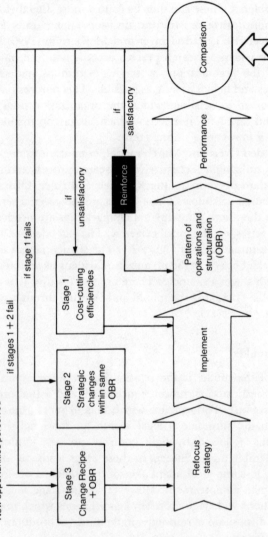

Figure 2.1 The extended Cyert and March model
Source: Adapted from Grinyer and McKiernan (1990)

underlying cultural pattern. It is more likely that the corporate organization will look to expand its existing market for existing products geographically, attempt to innovate on existing products or produce closely related products for the same market. But, where this stage is inadequate to cope with the growing mismatch between the activities of the organization and environmental conditions, actual performance deteriorates still further.

In order to cure the decline in performance, a fundamental change in the total organization activities is now necessary. This requires changing the OBR – the way the organization 'does business'. This can be achieved by either an externally or internally generated crisis which normally means a change in the composition of the dominant coalition, in particular, the chief executive officer. It is the top mangement team, at the centre and/or in the divisions, that personify this structured way of doing things which is no longer appropriate for the circumstances. The current OBR has to be smashed. Only this form of dramatic action can lead to the closure of the gap between aspiration levels and actual performance.

Learning through systematic planning

Strategic planning, as a higher-level learning rule, enters the model at each stage. It helps locate the best local solution through, for example, SWOT analysis at stage 1; helps to orchestrate a wider search for strategic responses at stage 2 without changing the existing OBR; and, finally, by signalling the inadequacies of the current OBR in dealing with the deterioration of performance it may contribute to the monitoring of pressure internally for change through dissatisfaction and lack of confidence. This may instil support for a 'revolution' in the dominant coalition and replacement of some or all of it, and facilitate the acceptance of major changes by a new CEO.

CORPORATE RECOVERY AND ORGANIZATIONAL DECISION MAKING

The model of organizational decision making developed in the previous section can now be placed in the context of corporate recovery. To link theory to practice, the general decision-making model is confronted by data collected in the UK manufacturing companies between 1982 and 1987 in a government-sponsored attempt to spread the lessons of recovery more fully around corporations in the UK economy. A total of twenty-six manufacturing businesses were studied in great detail over this period, involving over two hundred managerial interviews during a 5-year period.[7]

Recovery classifications

In a previous section, the difficulty of classifying corporate recoveries was noted. With the new research data, which takes into account both the turnaround and other recovery situations, it is now possible to attempt a classification. This is done based upon the organizations' 'distance' from failure. In Figure 2.2, these distances are denoted by early, intermediate and late. The latter category is similar to the turnaround situation.

Across the actual performance paths of these three recovery

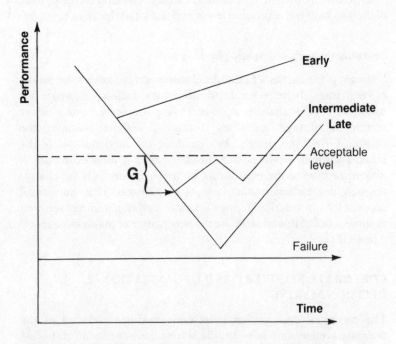

Figure 2.2 Actual and acceptable levels of performance of early, intermediate and late recoverers
Source: Grinyer *et al.* (1988)

stages are drawn two horizontal lines. The solid line represents a state of failure. To pass through it is to die. The hatched line represents the acceptable level of performance derived from the aspirational levels which are at the heart of the Cyert and March model and the extension of it. They represent that level of performance that is acceptable to managers given past performance, performance targets, performance of competitors and stakeholders' (e.g. investment analysts) expected performance. The idea behind illustrating both the actual performance path and the acceptable level is to emphasize the approaching negative gap between them or the negative gap itself (e.g. G, acceptable is greater than actual) which is instrumental in triggering change. Organizations are simply coalitions of individuals, and get stuck in the same sort of ruts and behaviour patterns. They need triggers to shock them out of this type of complacency or lethargy. The model argues that it is the interconnectedness between acceptable and actual performance that triggers even the lethargic management into taking action. The three stages of the recovery classification are early, intermediate and late.

Early

This stage represents those organizations in relative decline whose performance is above the acceptable level. Such organizations are anticipatory rather than reactive and make incremental, operational or strategic changes to reverse decline (see Nadler and Tushman 1989). The very thought that performance will fall below a level that is unacceptable provides a sufficient trigger to induce corrective action. These organizations could continue trading in their environments, sometimes quite successfully, for long periods. They are far removed from any threat of extinction. This typology of corporate recovery is adequately accommodated by the extended Cyert–March decision-making model in Figure 2.1. Organizations have moved quickly through stage 1 to stage 2, acknowledging that action at stage 1 (e.g. cost cutting) would probably not be sufficient alone to halt the relative decline quickly. Some organizations may move directly from their current domain to stages 2 or 3, effectively by-passing stage 1, by switching their resources into alternative product markets. Organizations of this kind are likely to contain proactive managers whose self-esteem and pride will be seriously damaged by any thoughts of average or below-average performance. They anticipate events and rectify matters early. They are likely to be risk takers rather than risk aversers. They are clearly 'winners' with high levels of actualization and achievement. Moreover, at this early stage, they have the time to think about how to recover and are not hurried by the threats of bankruptcy. Cash flows are also likely to be sufficiently positive to facilitate redirection.

Intermediate

These organizations have witnessed actual performance breaching the acceptable level and passing beneath it. This triggers alarm signals. The delay in reacting to the breach could be caused by an over-reliance on historically based accounting systems, (e.g. annual accounts that are typically found in small and medium-sized enterprises). It may be one or two quarters before reporting information reveals any problems of substance. At this stage there is a great temptation to blame poor actual performance on external factors. Management teams could be a mix of proactive and reactive, but are generally competent. Theirs is the traditional, sequential reaction to crisis.

Actions are taken at stage 1 of the extended Cyert and March model, e.g. controls are tightened, that induce a short-run improvement in performance. These actions could be in response to symptoms of the problem, rather than the problem itself and hence adverse performance sets in again. A wider search process is then employed for a solution and these organizations move through stage 2 and, possibly, stage 3 of the extended Cyert and March model. Once again they have some time to spare that enables the conventional model to operate well in its sequential way. Eventually, real problems are solved by, say, product-market switching and recovery should follow.

Late

At the intermediate stage, cost-cutting remedies may well be an appropriate solution to, what are perceived to be, external causes of decline. The decline process is full of such personal perceptions. It is wrapped up in individual psychology, notably pride. For research of this type, a general process of decline between the intermediate and late stages can be pieced together that reflects individual and organizations' response to crisis.

At this stage, we witness a refusal to accept blame. This is placed upon external factors such as import penetration or high interest rates. For organizations that slip beyond this stage, the pattern becomes more deceitful. As the negative gap grows and cost cutting and other tactics fail to work, the real crisis is denied. The truth is frequently adjusted and concealed, for instance, by the window dressing of the corporate accounts or by optimistic speeches from the chairman that aim to shore up the share price. Internal managerial morale deteriorates and good managers leave as performance fails to pick up and the constant denials and cover-ups attack their moral values. Ironically, the very people capable of turning the organization around, with their different ways of doing business, now depart in frustration since the old OBR which is running the organization is fixed and seemingly immovable. The crisis deepens and the costs of recovery escalate as resources are depleted through consistently negative cash flows. As the delay in breaking the old OBR and introducing new ways of doing business is prolonged, disintegration can occur and failure becomes a real possibility. More managers then leave. Beyond a certain point, top management teams sticking to their now outmoded ways of doing business cannot or will not see their full plight. Fortunately, this is witnessed externally by bankers or financial institutions who have, by this stage, had enough. External intervention is likely to follow, together with the removal of the dominant coalition (and their existing OBRs are smashed) and the introduction of new top management with new recipes for running the business. Hambrick and D'Aveni (1988) have appropriately referred to corporate declines of this type as 'downward spirals'.

The classification of recovery into early, intermediate and late is made up of anticipating (mostly early) and reactive (mostly intermediate and late) organizations. Grinyer and McKiernan (1990) have recently examined the conditions facing, and the characteristics of, these organizations in an attempt to form more robust categories of recovery. These are presented in Table 2.1.

RESEARCH RESULTS

The discussion below centres around the results in Tables 2.1 and 2.2.

Table 2.1 Characteristics of stages of recovery: causes, triggers and actions

Variable	Stages of recovery		
	Early %	Intermediate %	Late %
Causes			
Market decline	25	55	75
Financial	25	55	67
Project failure	25	36	75
Strategic problems	0	9	25
Poor marketing	75	9	8
Triggers			
Internal	75	100	54
External	25	0	46
Ownership threat	50	0	42
New CEO	25	36	33
Management sees problems			
Management sees opportunities	100	0	0
Actions			
Rationalization/closure	25	46	67
Changes in structure	25	46	50
Improved marketing	75	9	33
New product/market	75	18	58

Early stage results

Companies taking actions early had, predictably, fewer causes of decline (2.5) on average than organizations taking actions to recover at a later stage of decline (cf. 3.5 for intermediate and 3.9 for late). The most frequent cause of decline at this stage was poor marketing. Given that 75 per cent of them were in consumer products (Table 2.2), this was a crucial weakness. Feedback from pricing and advertising decisions was frequently short-term and such operational, functional maladies can usually be remedied by administrative changes as long as quality and consumer purchasing power remain strong. Internal triggers, especially the role of visionary or anticipatory existing management teams, were largely responsible for the appropriate remedies. These included improvements in marketing and more important the largest change in product market focus of any of the groups classified. These organ-

Table 2.2 Characteristics of stages of recovery: contextual variables

Variable		Early %	Stages of recovery Intermediate %	Late %
Industry	Growth	25	0	17
Life	Maturity	50	55	58
Cycle	Decline	25	45	25
Main	Consumer	75	46	33
Buyer	Industrial	25	54	66
Type				
Rate of decline		Very low	Medium	Medium
Size		Small/medium	Small/medium	Small/medium
Market share		Low	Medium	Medium
Industry concentration		Low	Low	Medium
Exit barriers		Low	Medium	High
Recovery rate		Low	Medium	Medium

izations are clearly in a position to make quick operational adjustments or strategic reorientations. This was helped as they faced low
exit barriers and were in fragmented industries (where innovation
may not be quickly followed by competitors). They also experienced
much lower rates of decline than the other groups. The interaction
of this group of variables was significant in facilitating complete re-
orientations in product-market scope. Such dramatic changes are
rare and organizations need the time and conditions necessary to
carry them through successfully. Their recoveries were sharp but
not dramatically so.

The motivating triggers for the actions taken of these earlier
recoveries is important. Acceptable levels of performance were
raised in half these organizations by threats of takeover (the
largest proportion of any stage). This stimulus provoked existing
management into a positive, anticipatory mode. This prompted
wider search procedures and shocked even relatively safe
organizations into major changes to the status quo. Remaining
organizations in this category were quite prosperous and had no
threat of immediate takeover, but significantly it was a chance
perception of major new opportunities that stimulated top management to raise their sights.

CASE EXAMPLE: JOHN WOOD GROUP

The recovery of the John Wood Group in Aberdeen, Scotland, is a typical member of these early recoveries. The organization ran a traditional fishing fleet with associated support facilities out of a harbour that was destined to become the oil capital of Europe. Members of the management team had been on holiday/business trips to the USA and had visited Texas. They witnessed at first hand the major impact that oil had had on the structure of industry. This event triggered ideas of product-market switching and diversification in their own family business. On their return to Scotland, they phased the transfer of their assets from the declining North Sea fishing industry to oil-related off-shore support services. They had a common knowledge of shipping and an asset base in the existence of warehousing and dock facilities that could be transferred into an alternative use. Such a dramatic switch is rare in family dominated companies. Yet the nature of share ownership (concentrated in the family) and the nature of the decision-making power (concentrated in family managers at the top of the organization), were instrumental in facilitating such a rapid and risky shift. The trigger in this case was the wider business experience that challenged their views not only of new ways of 'doing business' but also of new businesses to be involved in. This perception of new opportunities for more or less the same bundle of non-specific assets and the pro-active, risk-taking, managerial style enabled John Wood to out-perform the sector, subsequently, for many years. How many more businesses can break the mould and use their assets to attack new opportunities?

Intermediate stage results

Causes of decline in the intermediate class were more numerous and less operational than in the earlier group. Poor marketing was less of a problem than major market decline. Many of the industries had matured or were in decline with the resulting problems of excess capacity and financial difficulty. Risky projects that went wrong, through poor control, accelerated the plight of these organizations. The triggers for action were all internal to the organization. Management perceived the gravity of its problems in a reactive way as actual performance fell below what was considered to be acceptable. These managers planned the succession of their own chief executive officers where this was deemed appropriate. The absence of threatened takeovers as an external stimulus to increase managerial aspiration levels, is consistent with mature or declining markets, entry to which is less attractive to other firms seeking expansion by acquisition.

Against a background of relatively greater market decline, these intermediate organizations had larger market shares and faced higher exit barriers than the earlier group of recoverers. However, industry concentration was low which would suggest a lower likelihood of competitor reactions to major changes. As predicted in the extended Cyert-March model in Figure 2.1, their reactive stance was largely to try to achieve an acceptable level of performance within their current markets by means of rationalization and cost cutting. In effect, stage 1 changes were implemented within their existing OBRs. Consistently with this emphasis on rationalization, they tended to change their structures in the direction of greater centralization, providing a trimmed-down head office with greater decision-making power and a closer monitoring of costs. Only in isolated cases was there evidence of any strategic reorganizations. Because the financial impact of rationalization and cost-cutting is fairly immediate, recovery rates were faster than in the earlier group. A typical example of a company in the intermediate group is William Collins.

CASE EXAMPLE: WILLIAM COLLINS PLC

William Collins was a long-standing, family-managed printing and publishing company based in Glasgow, Scotland. It had large market shares in some areas of the publishing market such as bibles and dictionaries. It moved from old city-centre premises in the early 1970s to a new factory in a greenfield site on the outskirts of the city. This move created pressures and tensions among the largely female workforce who had developed strong social support groups in the old, but inefficient, multi-storey premises. They could no longer visit the shops at lunch time and their travel time to work was longer. Moreover, instead of taking the opportunity to re-equip the new factory with machines incorporating the latest technology, management merely transferred the old equipment to the new site. In addition, costs were a significant cause of decline. The historically low wages of the female labour force were rising with the advent of equal-pay legislation in the UK. Furthermore, the new factory had been financed with loans and, as interest rates climbed in the late 1970s, the company began to feel the squeeze.

These problems were compounded by a fundamental weakness in top and middle management. Collins had many of the succession problems associated with family-run businesses, where key managerial positions are reserved for family members who may not be as effective as their predecessors. The trigger for change was an internal recognition by management of its dangerous financial position (actual performance well below acceptable levels). A non-family CEO replaced the family incumbent after bitter and hostile board-room politics, thus breaking the existing OBR and introducing new recipes for doing business. This major change was accompanied by a heavy rationalization programme (50 per cent labour-force reduction), tighter production and quality control and the closure and sale of expensive head offices. In fact, as a powerful reminder to the employees of its financial plight, part of the remaining offices were bricked off to save rate payments.

Collins experienced a dramatic recovery based upon increased productivity, larger investments in new technology and a more open management style. The success of its sustained recovery attracted predators and in 1988 Collins was taken over.

Late stage results

Organizations at the late stage face relatively sharp declines in their industries, which were mainly in the mature or decline phases of their life cycle (see Table 2.2). Unfortunately, the high exit barriers confronting them prevented immediate divestment. Any improvement in performance was made manifestly more difficult by the high levels of industry concentration which tend to induce competitor infighting for market share as the industry decline spirals downwards. Moreover, these later recoverers faced multiple and more major structural problems than those of the previous two stages. Major declines in their markets were compounded by failure of big projects with the resultant worsening of their financial problems. Actual performance was far below that which was perceived to be acceptable by most internal and external groups. Hence, the triggers for action were both the threat of extinction and the threat of take-over. Interventions were initiated by dissatisfied bankers and/or institutional shareholders which enabled dramatic action to be taken in a large (42 per cent) number of cases. A new CEO was also an important stimulus as it was in the previous two groups.

Significantly, however, managements facing the threat of extinction were prepared to move from their old structured programmes (OBRs) having perceived the gravity of the problems facing them. Their actions involved both strategic and operating changes (see Hofer 1980): namely, heavy cost cutting, rationalization and closure (67 per cent); improved marketing in the hope of capturing an increased market share of the declining overall market (33 per cent); and strategic product market switches in nearly 60 per cent of the companies.

As was the case for organizations in the intermediate group, and common in turnaround strategies (Slatter 1984), those companies which were decentralized tended to move towards a centralized organizational structure to facilitate recovery. Autocratic management styles are frequently better at the turnaround stage. They enable decisions to be taken with greater haste in the context of a clear, if personified, corporate vision. However, significant research (Grinyer, Mayes and McKiernan 1988; Pettigrew and Whipp 1990), has now shown that once the organization has been turned around and has been on a successful track for two or three years, the style of management must shift away from autocracy and more towards democracy. In reality, this means another change in the chief executive from autocrat to democrat. The democrat must then steer the organization through a consensus-based consolidation phase lasting up to 4 or 5 years. Beyond that the second spur for growth must come from a more risk-taking, entrepreneurial-type manager.

The combination of operating and strategic measures used at the late stage, although not fully synchronized, was clearly related to the circumstances facing each organization. Clearly, organizations did more things and did them at the same time. In terms of the extended Cyert-March model this means that they are considering stage 1, 2 and 3 options almost in parallel, taking whatever actions are necessary to address their individual circumstances. This could give rise to the perception of a host of piecemeal measures rather than the existence of a coherent internally consistent recovery gestalt (see Hambrick and Schecter 1983) in what is effectively a turn-around situation. The recovery at Fisons is a classic example.

CASE EXAMPLE: THE FISONS STORY

By the late 1970s, Fisons faced an increase in competition in their traditional industry of fertilizers from much larger players such as ICI, which had greater economies of scale. Sales and profits suffered and Fisons, with poor financial controls, witnessed an escalation in its debt to dangerous levels. Unfortunately, despite the fact that senior management had realized for some considerable time that the medium- and long-term future of its fertilizer and agrochemical businesses was poor, Fisons had not moved away from these strategically weak business areas. Managerial, strategic and other sunk costs had created immobility. The financial situation eventually became so dire that the company began to trade at a loss in the early part of the 1980s. At the same time, the existing chairman reached retirement age and was succeeded by a widely regarded, dynamic leader. Subsequently, Fisons merged their agrochemical industries with Boots plc in a 50/50 deal. They sold off loss-making businesses and those with poor prospects (fertilizers). They acquired new businesses in strategically healthy areas (e.g. scientific instruments). They improved their management-accounting and cost-control systems and rationalized their top management team. Head office was slimmed down and strategic planning (as a higher-level learning rule) was introduced. Although the company centralized initially to force through the recovery, it decentralized as soon as this turn-around was consolidated to give the divisions all but strategic autonomy. Fisons had therefore addressed cost cutting, product-market switching and strategic re-orientations in parallel. A new recipe for 'doing business' had stimulated recovery.

PERFORMANCE OF THE MODEL

The results provide valuable support for the extended Cyert and March model of Figure 2.1. Actions taken fall into categories of tighter control, adjustment of strategy without fundamental change in OBRs, or more fundamental change in strategy involving the adoption of new 'recipes'. The model however predicts that these will occur as sequential events. In practice, at the early and late stages in particular, they occurred in parallel. Pro-active management, determined to improve performance, controlled existing businesses more tightly; took steps to improve their strategic posture whilst staying within the current OBR; divested businesses they did not understand, or where they were competitively weak and so contracting back to core-business; and, sometimes, at the same time, diversified by acquisition into related or even unrelated businesses.

However, the underlying assumptions of the model such as a comparison between aspiration levels and their manifestation in terms of acceptable levels of performance suits the data well. The importance of structured ways of 'doing business' (OBRs), survives intact from its confrontation with the data. First, changes in strategy are less frequent than steps to improve current performance (e.g. differentiation, export-market entry). These are essentially strategic re-adaptations rather than fundamental changes. Organizations tend to preserve their existing OBRs as long as possible, and any changes are minor. Second, when fundamental strategic change occurred it took two forms. The most popular occurrence was a return to a well-understood core business, a sale of assets or a harvesting of weaker businesses. So organizations reinforced their core OBRs by disposing of areas in which they were no longer applicable. In the rare event where fundamental change involved new OBRs, this was done mainly through acquisitions. Organizations bought into new OBRs in the form of human organizations, structuration, beliefs, conventions, operating plant, procedures and networks of relationships of the new business which they were entering. This amounts to 'buying in' an applied version of the recipe of the industry entered.

These acquisitions represent a quicker route to adopting new OBRs without imposing threats to existing ones, as acquired companies can be 'bolted-on' to existing corporate structures. Hence, the new OBRs need not clash with the old. Some old OBRs may still be relatively successful and so they can survive without destruction in such a system. Unsuccessful parts of old OBRs are allowed to fade away, as the new ones gain wider acceptance or are disposed of as businesses in which they are embodied are divested. This is a more efficient route to adopting new OBRs than the internal one of changing the CEO and driving change from within (see Grinyer and Spender 1979). Hence, it is possible to achieve major change without the trauma of discarding the old OBR. However, this was not always the case. In Fisons, the fertilizer and agricultural business as described earlier, which had been the core, was sold off. In Sidlaw Industries, the traditional core textile business was shrunk to a minimum. At Associated Paper Industries, the number of paper mills was reduced from 7 to 1 during the 1970s while the firm expanded into more specialized, higher-margin business. So fundamental rejection of the OBR is sometimes necessary, particularly so in mature or declining businesses.

Overall, it is clear that decline, especially at the late/turnaround stage is a multi-faceted process (Zimmerman 1986) and the inter-action of the many causes is a complicated feature. This means that co-ordinated actions need to be taken on a number of fronts yielding a number of custom-made recovery strategies (Ramanujam 1984). This is a crucial result as it explains, to some extent, why authors like Hambrick and Schecter (1983) found huge clusters of 'piece-meal' turnaround strategies. It can appear that companies in crises do lots of things all at once.

At later stages of decline, adjustments to structure from de-centralized to centralized appear to facilitate immediate recovery in this UK sample (compare this with Melin's (1985) Scandinavian sample which, perhaps because of the number of international businesses, involved a more decentralized structure during recovery). Moreover, not all recovery strategies in our sample involved complete replacements of chief executive officers or top management teams in an attempt to break old programmes/practices (see also the work of Biteman (1979) and O'Neill (1986) where, in virtually all turnaround cases, top management was replaced in these US-based studies).

It is useful to emphasize the changing nature of the triggers for action between the early, intermediate and late recovery groups. In the early groups, the threat of takeover or the perception of major new opportunities was sufficient to induce change before multiple causes of decline became serious. In the intermediate stages, existing management's reactive response (possibly due to an over-reliance on historic accounting data) was sufficient, given the presence of good diagnostic qualities without complete changes in the nature of the business or its programmes. Later on, however, in what is more of a turnaround situation the threat of extinction together with threats of takeover seems to trigger existing manage-ment into breaking their old programmes and practices as survival instincts take over. Changes in top management and the introduc-tion of new CEO are important but not necessarily sufficient in altering these OBRs. Internal management teams, given sufficient stresses from external threats, can break their own templates on how to do business.

Hence, it is important in studying recoveries to be able to identify the stage of recovery in particular as this relates to the gap, whether positive or negative, between actual and acceptable levels of performance. The opportunities and threats at each stage are clearly different. The actions required for a sustained recovery are different at each stage. It is easier to engineer recovery situations if existing OBRs remain intact. This reduces the level of internal conflict and eases the political process. At early stages, operational changes and strategic changes are clearly possible within existing OBRs. At later stages the multiplicity of causes of decline, their interactions and the steepness of decline usually leads to the breaking of OBRs and emergency actions having to be taken on all fronts.

It is therefore very difficult to generalize about this later extinction-driven phase. Each recovery strategy seems to be specific to the organization involved. Existing management teams must realize that their 'way of doing business' is now obsolete. They must recognize it is now time to let go. Their own programmes and templates have prevented major change taking place up to this crisis point. The later this change is left, the more costly it is in capital and human terms.

Table 2.3a Common causes of decline

Causes

Internal (67%[1])
- Management defects:
  autocratic leaders; poor succession programmes; lack of balance in top teams (e.g. too many engineers); lack of middle management depth; lack of participative boards.
- Management errors of omission:
  lack of proper budgetary and cost controls; price not reflective of cost base, failure to respond to market changes especially competitive ones.
- Management errors of commission:
  overexpansion of products; facilities and personnel beyond firm's resources.

External (33%[1]) (in order of importance)
- Decline in government demand or change in regulations
- Increased foreign competition
- Economic variables, e.g. inflation, interest rates or merger activity leading to larger competition
- Change in government regulations or demand
- Changes in demographic/social variable
- Changes in product technology

Note: [1]Estimates from Bibeault (1982)

BLENDING THEORY AND PRACTICE: THE 'HOW TO' LITERATURE

The previous section has emphasized the importance of understanding the nature of the process of decision-taking in organizations and also of recognizing the organization's position relative to decline, given the relationship between its *actual* and *acceptable* levels of performance.

It is useful to interpret the closely related literature on corporate turnaround, succinctly summarized by Hoffman (1989), with these two crucial issues in mind. There has been a great deal of research work in corporate turnarounds over the last fifteen years. Corporate turnarounds became front page news in the 1980s, as large companies all over the world had to engage in turnaround strategies, e.g. ICL Computers, Dunlop and BSR in the UK, Peugeot, Waterman and SAS in Continental Europe and Westinghouse Control Data, Walt Disney Company and United Airlines in the USA. It is clear that in each individual situation the causes of decline are so different that the strategies adopted are almost as varied. Hence, it is important to have a thorough understanding of the processes that have been discussed in the previous sections to be able to formulate a successful recovery strategy.

The 'how to' literature, however, is important for reinforcing some of the results already presented. But care must be taken in the interpretation of its results for a number of reasons. First, it is rare for the causes reported to have been statistically related to decline or for the research to be of sufficient rigour to have established the validity of the external causes as real issues rather than hooks on which inefficient management has been able to blame the corporation's demise. Second, no attention is given to the links between the causes of decline and the remedying actions taken or the relationship between actual performance and acceptable performance which is a forceful and significant trigger for these actions. Finally, the nature of the decision-making process and the role of belief systems, values and cultures that form managerial templates or programmes is rarely discussed.

However, this 'how to' literature is useful in its identification of a common cause of decline (see Table 2.3a) and the five generic strategies adopted by organizations in recovery situations (see Table 2.3b). These gestalts rely on the common distinction between operating and strategic strategies already discussed. Hoffman (1989) segments these five strategies into three stages, representing their suggested sequence of implementation. The preparatory stage includes the strategy of restructuring leadership and organizational culture. The short-term fix stage includes three operating strategies: cost reduction, asset redeployment and selected product-market pruning. The growth stage emphasizes repositioning of the product-market focus. This time ordering of actions is consistent with the results of more rigorous, academically based research (Grinyer, Mayes and McKiernan 1988; Pettigrew and Whipp 1990; 1991). Although Hoffman (1989) is keen to emphasize that not all organizations involved in recovery situations need go through all three stages nor use all of the strategies at each stage. Most strategies employed defensive (stemming decline) and offensive (improvement performance) activities. These generic turnaround strategies are displayed in Table 2.3b.

Restructure leadership and organization culture

Strong leadership seems to be one of the most important factors cited for successful turnarounds. Any leadership change usually occurred during the preparatory stages but other structural and cultural changes persisted during the turnaround cycle through the short-term fix stage to the growth stage. These leadership changes seem to be made for both symbolic and substantive reasons. It is argued that replacing managers stimulates change by altering current attitudes, breaking mind sets, removing concentrations of power, and providing a new strategic vision for the oganization to follow. This fits in well with the processes described in the last section. However, even the bulk of this literature would seem to agree that the complete replacement of top management is not necessary to orchestrate a recovery. For example, the extent to which top management was replaced varied from 33 to 100 per cent in all the research studies investigated by Hoffman. Moreover, the notion of changes in formal organizational structures from decentralization to centralization in order to concentrate decision authority during the recovery situation seems commonplace. The difficult issue for many of the executives managing turnaround situations seems to be in the facilitation of cultural change. In many instances defensive cultural changes focused upon loosening the old culture and breaking up power bases, for example, by changes in leadership. These were coupled by offensive attempts at cultural

Table 2.3b Five generic strategies of recovery (adapted from Hoffman 1989)

Strategy	Types of action	Suitable conditions
I Restructure leadership and organization/culture	• Replace top manager(s)	• Causes for turnaround internal • Need to diversify out of industry
	• Use temporary structures • Alter organization structure	• Control and communications problems • Facilitate repositioning • Culture change
	• Alter culture	• Structural change
II Cost reduction	• Reduce expenses • Institute controls	• Internal causes of decline • Sales 60–80 per cent of breakeven
II Asset redeployment	• Sell assets • Shutdown or relocate units	• Over expansion/low capacity use • Sales 30–60 per cent of breakeven • Rapid technological change • Rapid entry of new competitors
II Selective product/market strategy	Defensive: • Decrease marketing efforts • Divest products Offensive: • Increase marketing efforts • Increase prices • Improve quality, service	• Over expansion • Causes for turnaround external • High capacity use • Possessing operating and strategic weaknesses
III Repositioning	Defensive: • Niche • Market penetration • Decrease price • Divest products	• Overexpansion (defensive) • Improved short-run profitability • Causes for turnaround

Table 2.3b Continued

Strategy	Types of action	Suitable conditions

	Offensive:
	• Diversification into
	  new products
		external
		• Major decline in
		  market share
		• Non-diversified firms
		  faced with external
		  causes of decline
		  (offensive)

change by re-orientating employees' cognitive maps, for example by coaching, outside training, building shared goals, and emphasizing the successful attributes of the previous OBRs. The organizational structural changes were designed to elicit the desired cultural rejuvenation.

Cost reduction strategies

The defensive tactics of reducing expenses, receivables, inventory levels and personnel is a clear signal that management means business. It is argued that controlling costs is the key to successful turnaround. It is the offensive cost-reduction strategies that lay the foundation for successful recovery. Hence the introduction of proper management controls, for example budgetary, the introduction of strategic planning (high-level learning rules), and proper and efficient management information systems delivered by the latest information technology (computers) is essential to any recovery strategy adopted.

Asset redeployment strategies

The improvements in capacity utilization and employee productivity were normally achieved by large asset redeployment strategies. Hofer (1980) argues that companies in dire financial circumstances should only retain those assets that would be used over the next 2 years: hence instrumental defensive activities included the sale of assets, the closure of plant or closing branch operations. The offensive redeployment strategies included relocating plants to gain better cost advantages and the merger of branch operations.

Selected product-market strategies

These strategies involve short-run changes in the firm's marketing mix and are mostly aimed at increasing sales revenue and hence inventory turnover which seem to form the basis of successful as opposed to unsuccessful turnarounds. The defensive strategies include reducing marketing expenses or harvesting/divesting parts of the product portfolio. Bibeault (1982) suggested that companies in turnaround situations should focus on the top 20 to 30 per cent of their most profitable products. The offensive strategy involved the increasing of prices, promotion, quality and customer services.

Repositioning strategies

It is these strategies that reflect the second set of actions identified by the work of Grinyer, Mayes and McKiernan (1988) and Pettigrew and Whipp (1990) referred to earlier. They are aimed at sustaining the recovery situation from the short term to the medium and long terms. Essentially, once the firm is clear of its financial crisis a repositioning or refocusing of its mission is usually essential. The new vision is often supplied by a new CEO or combined top management team (Pettigrew and Whipp 1990) or, as has been established earlier, can be generated internally from existing management teams who see the need to change the way they do business. Defensive activities involve repositioning the firm on the basis of its core business activities. This involved the divestment of products and divisions that did not fit the new definition of the firm. In this instance, the firm may hang on to its existing OBR, slicing off those parts of the organization for which the OBR is no longer appropriate. Offensive repositioning activities involved diversification efforts to expand product lines or entry to new business areas via acquisition, organic growth, strategic alliance or vertical integration. Clearly, across these studies, acquisitions seem to be the most important route for a diversification away from old product-market areas. They enable new recipes and new OBRs to enter the organization. Most repositioning strategies involve both defensive and offensive moves requiring the organization to continually re-structure as new divisions (and new OBRs) are added.

IMPLICATIONS FOR MANAGEMENT

There is a wealth of pragmatic literature on how to turn organizations round. This stems largely from consultants and executives involved in these activities. The implications for management shown below are derived from a combination of many of the academic research programmes tempered by this consultancy expertise.

1   Managers need to select and monitor financial and behavioural criteria relevant for indicating declining trends in the operation or strategic performance of their organization. Quarter-by-quarter management is re-active and essentially short-term, measuring only financial health. Strategic health requires a longer-term view and proactive management.

2   During the process of relative decline it is imperative to establish at an early stage whether sufficient management talent and, in particular, leadership exists to manage the impending crisis and recovery. How structured is management in its way of doing business? Will this incommode the recovery?

3   The CEO needs to establish a reliable top management team to manage the turnaround. This team needs to have access to precise information on the causes of decline and to subject this to systematic analysis and interpretation.

4   Management should formulate a two-stage plan. The first stage is aimed at stemming the decline and generating positive cash flows and improvements in profitability over the short term. The second stage involves repositioning the organization with the aim of sustaining the short-run recovery into the medium and long term. The first-phase actions are normally operating ones and the second-stage actions are normally strategic ones.

5   Implementing the stage changes above, requires a reformulation of the strategic mission and consequent organization restructuring. A crucial feature here is the managing of change relating to existing organizational cultures, and the need for positive motivational techniques that ensure a winning attitude is developed within the organization.

At base, each organization, as a group of individuals, has a unique composition. Moreover, it faces a unique combination of external factors that bear upon it at any one time. In a period of relative decline the extent of crisis that is real or imaginary and the reactions to that crisis within the organization will be different in each case. Hence, it is almost impossible to

specify a single turnaround gestalt. However, a clear understanding of the way that organizations develop, the way they
take decisions, the underlying process that creates the trigger for
them to take action, and a broad specification of the stages of
recovery should help individual managers to cope with their
immediate situation. There is one lesson that stands out from all
this research. Those companies that acted early were able to
formulate a greater number of possible options and sustain their
success for longer periods. In addition, they incurred less costs
in human and organization terms. Hence, the emphasis must be
placed on active environmental monitoring and early, appropriate reactions.

SUMMARY

This chapter began with an introduction to the problems authors
have had in classifying turnaround situations such that generic turnaround strategies become difficult to prescribe. To clarify the
position, the discussion centred upon the way organizations make
decisions. This theoretical section was then tied into the nature of
the corporate decline process and early, intermediate and late
recoveries were identified. The theory was then confronted with
research data and the characteristics of the three stages of recovery
were established, together with the manner in which the theoretical
model described reality. Finally, this match of theory and academic
research was linked into the salient results of the burgeoning literature
from practitioners on corporate recovery in an attempt to provide
guidance for readers experiencing these issues in their own
organizations.

Recovery may be a real option for the 'forgotten cell' of the
growth-share matrix. In particular, if, through structured OBRs, the
business has been allowed to decline, the situation has a good
chance of recovery if internal and external pressure can be brought
to bear in a serious attempt to change outmoded ways of 'doing
business'. The answer is to stay flexible and proactive.

Chapter 3

Internationalization

INTRODUCTION

International business exploded onto corporate and academic agendas during the 1980s. The growth in world trade began to significantly exceed the growth in world GNP around the mid 1950s. The growth in foreign direct investment (FDI) since the mid 1960s has been equally staggering. In fact Shell's chief economist, DeAnne Julius (1990) claimed that the volume of FDI was 'changing the structure of the world economy'. Between 1983 and 1988 FDI world-wide rose by more than 20 per cent annually – four times faster than world trade. By 1988, the worldwide stock of FDI assets by the G5 nations of USA, Japan, West Germany, Britain and France was a colossal $757 bn or 75 per cent of total world stock. Moreover, the local sales of foreign-owned firms in the USA was one and a half times larger than the country's imports in 1985. These sales account for more than half the USA's exports and a third of its imports. This monumental growth, largely fuelled by international liberalization – especially in the service sector, is concentrated in the industrial world (flows to developing countries fell in real terms during the 1980s). Hence, much of the traditional meaning of official merchandise trade and balance of payment statistics is significantly diluted as the sales and purchases of the FDIs effectively substitute for imports and exports. International business is clearly here to stay.

Internationalization can be an alternative to 'divestment' in the low-share, low-growth cell of the BCG matrix. It should be included on the wider list of strategic options generated for such businesses that can help avoid the boxing-in of strategic thought. There will be circumstances, perhaps characterized by declining markets or obsolete technology, that render international expansion redundant or ineffective as a strategy for sustaining improvements in performance beyond the short term. Furthermore, the heightened managerial capacity and vision necessary to ensure international competitiveness together with other inferior internal resources would mitigate against its selection. However, there are a number of circumstances where it would be both a credible choice and a credible option.

1   Low levels of national productivity, high unit-labour costs, shortages of skilled labour, fluctuations in energy costs and tough environmental control laws can all act to drive domestic costs upwards rendering competitiveness ineffectual against imports. Many of these reasons, coupled with a liberalization of exchange controls, have been behind the rapid FDIs of Swedish companies in the late 1980s and early 1990s, e.g. Skandia, Asea–Brown Boveri, Ericsson, Volvo, Procordia, Trelleborg and PLM. True, the proximity to a more liberalized EC market and the potentially lucrative new German market provided additional demand-side stimuli for their acquisitive behaviour.

2   Relatively small domestic markets (e.g. Scandinavian countries, Finland, the Netherlands) mean that competitive advantages lodged in economies of scale or scope are difficult to achieve. A wider market perspective is necessary. Hence, their indigenous organizations are often at the forefront of international operations, e.g. Electrolux, Pharmacia (Sweden). Taiwanese companies, tired of the shackles of original equipment manufacturing (OEM) and fuelled by a desire to expand beyond a limited and insular domestic market became internationally acquisitive in the late 1980s and early 1990s. Their acquisition of brand names, technology and distribution networks should enable them to penetrate foreign markets on their own, e.g. President Enterprises' $335 million acquisition of Wyndham Foods (third largest US biscuit company); China Rebar Group's £20 million purchase of Omni Bank of California; Acer's $100 million payment for Altos (US computer systems).

3   Saturated domestic markets, or those in recession, can provide their own stimuli for international expansion. In the former case, internationalization can provide a vehicle for continued growth. In the latter case, it provides a risk-hedging strategy, giving the security of a balanced portfolio.

   • Tube Investments (United Kingdom) had a strong hold

on the maturing UK domestic appliances market in the early 1980s. Corporate growth meant international expansion. This was facilitated by divesting a major part of its *successful* portfolio (cash cows and stars in domestic appliances) and concentrating on international acquisitions in the specialist engineering sector where it is now (1991) a world leader.

- In Scotland, the declining Dundee jute industry is coloured with examples of technological switching and international-ization (e.g. Don & Low) that enabled companies to recover sharply from stagnating as well as saturated markets.
- Troubled Taiwanese textile OEMs (above) are *together* seeking to acquire international brand names to facilitate foreign expansion from insular domesticity.

As the UK recession deepened by 1991, many successful companies were able to survive on the strength of their export sales: e.g. Alcoa (aluminium sheet for can ends in the drinks industry) with 90 per cent exports; Siliconix (semiconductor) with over 80 per cent exports; Butterley Brick (construction) – in the face of a drop in 1990 of demand domestically of 50 million bricks, Butterley improved exports to 30 million bricks, including 3 million bricks to Japan from the UK; while the high interest rates took their toll on domestic orientated companies.

Internationalization strategies can work, but they are neither easy nor quick. It should be emphasized that these strategies are not a short-term response to recessions or exchange-rate swings. They are complex, costly and risky. They are not a panacea for every business that has been called a dog. Off-loading spare capacity abroad is not the equivalent of an internationalization strategy.

An understanding of the internationalization process is essential for assessing the suitability of the strategy for each business.[1] This chapter provides a guide to the underlying theories of trade and invest-ment – the 'why' of the internationalization process. The 'how' of internationalization is covered through an examination of traditional and more recent entry modes. The final section concentrates on the 'where' of international business and provides more pragmatic guidelines to country selection.

An appreciation of the underlying theories provides a richness in our understanding of the why, how and where organizations engage in international business. As the study of international competitive-ness goes back centuries, the theories available are plentiful. Two of the strongest branches are the theories of international trade where the analysis focuses on the country, and of international investment, where the analysis focuses on the organization. Moreover, they are powerfully linked by Vernon (1966) in the product life cycle and together form the basis of much of the recent influential work of leading writers in international competitive strategy (Porter 1986; 1990; Ghoshal 1987; Ohmae 1990).

INTERNATIONAL TRADE THEORIES

Between 1500 and 1800, the prevailing doctrine of political economy and arguably the first theory of trade, was *mercantilism*. Simply, nations engaged in trade to maximize their wealth (or treasure) by maximizing the gap between exports and imports. This wealth accumulation, usually in gold, was spent in fortifying the military and developing national institutions, thereby consolidating the power of the central governments of the emerging nation states. Although it faded dramatically in popularity after the early 1800s, its legacies, especially terminology, can be witnessed in all types of modern states whose policy objectives include 'trade surpluses' (neo-mercantilism).[2] Indeed, the use of the oil-related revenue surpluses by Iraq to assemble one of the most formidable military forces in modern times, prior to the Gulf War, provides a chilling example.

Classical theory

Classicists were the first to establish the well known finding that 'trade results in a higher level of *economic* well-being for its participants than would be possible for them without it'. Their work, together with later extensions and developments, forms the basis of the modern trade, international business and global strategy literature. Hence, it is valuable to understand the original propositions developed by the three leading classical political economists – Adam Smith, David Ricardo and John Stuart Mill.

Nations trade because there are price differences between the same (or similar) goods in their countries. Classical theory assumes that these price differences are the direct result of cost differences[3] in production in the respective countries. These cost differences can be of two kinds – absolute and comparative.

Absolute costs[4]

Adam Smith in his *Wealth of Nations* (1776) proposed the theory of absolute advantage. He asserted that country wealth is reflected in the goods and services available for consumption by the citizens and not, as under mercantilist teaching, on the accumulation of treasure. This consumption would be maximized under free trade. Trade would occur because of cost differences between nations in production.

The cost structure of France and Scotland for the production of whisky and shoes is shown in Table 3.1. Scotland has an absolute cost advantage over France in the production of whisky (6 compared with 2 gallons per day) but France has the absolute cost advantage in shoes (12 to 10). If citizens of both countries want to consume both products, there is a clear basis for trade to occur.

Consider two possible options for satisfying demand.[5] If each country has 100 employee days available, option 1 would involve devoting them to producing both products (say 50 days to each). The total output for both countries would amount to 400 gallons of whisky and 1,100 pairs of shoes a day. Option 2 involves the *specialization* of each country to the production of one of the products and subsequent trade to acquire the other. If each has 100 days available, the total output would be greater than that of option 1, i.e. 600 gallons of whisky produced by Scotland due to its absolute cost advantage and 1,200 pairs of shoes by France. Each country ends up producing that product for which it has a competitive advantage. These advantages, Smith suggested, are either given by nature to a country (climate, physical resources etc.) or are acquired (product or process know-how). The natural advantage explains much of the agriculturally dominated trade of Smith's day and the acquired

Table 3.1 Absolute costs

	Employee output per		Option 1		Option 2	
	Whisky	Shoes	Whisky	Shoes	Whisky	Shoes
Scotland	6	10	300	500	600	—
France	2	12	100	600	—	1,200
Total			400	1,100	600	1,200

advantage is fundamental in explaining modern trade in manufactured goods.

Assuming that consumers in France and Scotland want both
products trade will occur. The terms of exchange will be influenced
by the relative intensity and price-responsiveness of demand by each
country for the other's product. Mill (1848) called this 'reciprocal
demand'. Simply, it means that in the likely event that the French
desire for Scotch whisky is greater than the Scots desire for French
shoes, the terms of trade will favour the Scots who can then push up
the rate of exchange of shoes for Scotch.

Comparative costs

David Ricardo (1817) expanded on Smith's absolute advantage
theory by asking what happens to trade if one country has absolute
advantages in both (or all) products? Will trade still go on? His
answer was yes. His explanation was given with reference to
comparative costs, i.e. the expression of the cost of a product in
relation to another. This can be shown if we stick to the same
example of Table 3.1 but modify the cost structure to give Scotland
a double advantage in both whisky and shoes (by dropping shoe
output from 12 to 8 in France). Table 3.2 summarizes this. Comparative costs are established for one product in terms of the other to
find out where respective advantages lie.

Comparative costs based on Table 3.2 are as follows:

1   In Scotland, a gallon of whisky costs (comparatively) $10 \div 6 =$
     1.66 pairs of shoes while in France, whisky costs $8 \div 2 = 4$ pairs
     of shoes. Scotland clearly has a comparative-cost advantage in
     the production of whisky.
2   In Scotland, a pair of shoes costs $6 \div 10 = 0.6$ gallons of

Table 3.2 Comparative costs

| | Output per employee day | |
	Whisky	Shoes
Scotland	6	10
France	2	8

whisky. In France shoes cost $2 \div 8 = 0.25$ gallons of whisky. France has a comparative-cost advantage in shoe production.

This result is an expected one since it can be established that if different internal cost ratios are present it is certain that each country will have a comparative advantage in one of the two products. As Weekly and Aggarwal (1987) emphasize:

> this axiom is the crux of both the theory and practice of international trade, because it reveals an almost limitless potential for countries to profit from trade with one another. Given the extremely high probability that different countries will not have exactly identical internal cost ratios, the prospects for mutually beneficial trade are likewise extremely high.

To verify the gains from trade, consider that Scotland would have to give up 60 gallons of whisky if it wanted to switch into a domestic production of 100 shoes (at a ratio of 0.6). So if it could get 100 shoes from France for less than 60 gallons all would be well. France, on the other hand, has to sacrifice 240 shoes to produce domestically, 60 gallons of whisky (at a ratio of 4). There is a broad base of opportunity for trade that would benefit each party, even though one of them can produce both products cheaper than the other.

Extension of classical theory

Hecksher-Ohlin

The simplified exposition above is at the root of the explanation of world trade. Both Smith and Ricardo showed how output can be increased by production specialization. The question remained as to why a country would be relatively more efficient in the production of certain goods – what is the source of comparative advantage? Two Swedish economists Eli Hecksher (1919) and Bertil Ohlin (1933) asserted that this was due to the differences in countries' endowments[6] of labour relative to those of land and capital.

A large labour pool, valuable oil reserves and rich arable land may be the blessings of three countries. Hecksher-Ohlin argued that countries will maximize the use of these abundant resources and specialize in related produce.

- A high-labour/low-land economy (e.g. Hong Kong, Netherlands, Taiwan) regardless of its physical resources would

operate labour-intensive production (e.g. clothing and elec-
tronics in multi-storey factories that minimize land use in Hong
Kong and Singapore; another example is the reintroduction in
1991 of labour-intensive production of the Morris Minor car in
Sri Lanka, twenty years after it had been discontinued from its
British production base). A low-labour/high-land economy (e.g.
Turkey, Canada, Australia) would specialize in produce that
maximizes land use (e.g. sheep, wheat).

• A high-labour/low-capital economy (e.g. India, Iran, Tunisia)
would specialize in labour-intensive produce (e.g. hand-made
carpets).

For economies endowed with rich capital assets (e.g. USA, Japan,
Canada) the Hecksher-Ohlin theory would predict that their exports
would consist of capital-intensive produce. Unfortunately, Leontief
(1954), followed by other economists, found that exports from the
USA, Japan and Canada were labour-intensive relative to imports.
This 'Leontief paradox' has been explained by the marked difference in the level of labour-force skills between nations. The smaller
US labour component relative to its rich capital assets is a highly
skilled one; this may give the USA a comparative advantage in
labour-intensive produce despite its capital endowments. However,
Leontief had overlooked the sunk capital component (in education
and training) that was contained in the US labour component. Once
stripped of this, Kenen (1965), Branson and Monoyios (1977) found
US exports to be capital-intensive as predicted by the Hecksher-
Ohlin theory.

PRODUCT LIFE CYCLE

Familiar to marketeers and every MBA participant, the product life
cycle (PLC) has been fruitfully used by Vernon (1966) to explain
both international trade *and* international investment. Lindner
(1961) has argued that the Hecksher-Ohlin theory explains trade
patterns in primary produce reasonably well. But comparative-
advantage based trade in manufactured products is determined not
only by factor endowments of countries but also by technology,
culture, education, government influences and other variables.
Hence, such trade will tend to be most active between countries of
similar profiles especially of consumer tastes and income, e.g. the
USA will trade in consumer goods with the UK, other Western and
European nations and Japan.

The PLC has been useful as an illustrative guide to this type of trade in manufactured goods and has also been successful in explaining the evolution of services. According to Vernon, the theory of comparative-cost advantage and factor endowments lacks realism. He places less emphasis on classical doctrine and more on innovation, the uncertainty of early product development and marketing, the cost implications of scale economies, oligopolistic rivalry and copying. The characteristics of the four familiar stages of the life cycle are given below:

Introduction

Product innovations[7] are most likely to be developed in response to domestic needs in high income, advanced nations, e.g. USA, France, Japan, UK, West Germany, where domestic demand is strong and R&D resources concentrated. The product is manufactured locally, feedback obtained from the market and consequent improvements made. Production expands to achieve scale economies and any excess capacity is exported to other 'similar profile' industrial countries. Before the product is standardized, production is essentially labour intensive, retaining a degree of flexibility to incorporate the changes from market feedback.

Growth

If successful, the product ought to enjoy rapidly increasing sales. The original monopoly position may be broken by competitors offering variants to escape patent litigation. Foreign market demand increases, exports remain profitable, while production cost savings from scale economies exceed transport costs and tariffs. At some stage the situation will go into reverse as foreign market demands expand even further. Direct investments will then take place in foreign countries and the output of those manufacturing plants will service, initially, local markets. The product starts to become more standardized and emphasis switches to improvements in the process technology.

Maturity

Worldwide demand begins to level off, forcing a shake-out among competitors. The product becomes highly standardized, and so cost becomes a major competitive weapon. Longer production runs improve scale economies and the consequent low unit costs and prices enable a wider market to open up for the product in the LDCs. The production advantages now shift from the innovating country to those LDCs where lower cost labour working on a standardized, capital-intensive work process is the key determinant of location.

Decline

Markets in advanced economies decline more rapidly than LDCs as income is switched to satisfy the insatiable demand of the affluent consumers for new products. All production of the original innovation is now based in the LDCs.

The product life-cycle predictions are borne out by early research and case evidence especially for automobiles, sewing machines, typewriters, tractors, synthetic materials and some electrical and electronic products (Lutz and Green 1983) making it a valuable extension of trade theory. In addition, it links strongly and intuitively to theories of foreign direct investment (see later). But, its applicability is limited for products with rapid innovations (short life cycles) e.g. product obsolescence in electronics, luxury goods where cost minimization is not a critical issue, goods with high transportation costs and products with high brand loyalty sustained through advertising and other differentiation strategies. However, more recently MNCs have tended to consider the joint introduction of production facilities in domestic and foreign markets and also budget for LDC product at a very early stage. Hence, although the PLC was extremely useful for explaining trade and investment patterns from the 1950s to the 1980s, the 1990s may present a different challenge. There is no doubt, however, that it made an enormous and dynamic contribution to the previous static comparative-advantage theories.

THEORIES OF FOREIGN DIRECT INVESTMENT

Foreign direct investment (FDI) by organizations can be a complex activity. The classic trade theories were good at explaining the movement of goods and services (trade). Equally the movement between countries of the resources required to produce those goods and services (FDIs) is explained by the classic theory of investment.

This assumes that each of these factors of production (e.g. labour, capital) will gravitate towards the highest return they can obtain. Hence, countries rich in capital resources, will invest capital abroad (e.g. USA, UK, Japan) and countries rich in labour resources will tend to witness an out-migration of labour (e.g. Egyptians and Indians to OPEC nations in the Middle East) which seek the highest reward in terms of wages. However, even the shift in theories from trade to factors of production fails to fully explain the complex foreign-investment decisions of individual organizations, especially since the Second World War.

A significant feature of this modern era has been the growth in *direct* as opposed to portfolio-type investments. The latter, involving investments in stocks, bonds or other securities and driven by differences in risk-adjusted interest rates between countries, is well explained by economists in long-established theories of international capital flows. Direct investments, by involving a bundle of firm-specific assets in labour, managerial skills, technological and production know-how alongside capital, is seen as a far more complicated phenomenon.

Traditional modes of entry to foreign markets

Penetration of a foreign market was traditionally considered to follow an incremental staging process from a specific firm-based advantage in the domestic market, through export enquiries, licensing, branches and eventually to investment in production resources in a foreign country (FDI). This process is shown in Figure 3.1. Much research has been conducted on the identification of the stimuli to start exporting that underpins the initial internationalization decision of organizations. These original export stimuli have been categorized into proactive and reactive (Olson and Wiedersheim-Paul 1978; Wiedersheim-Paul *et al.* 1978; Cavusgil and Nevin 1980).

1 *Proactive*: mostly internal-managerial, based upon excess capacity and/or distinctive competence. Rational, objective orientated behaviour.
2 *Reactive*: external stimuli such as unsolicited orders from foreign customers, entry of domestic competitors in foreign markets, increased competition in domestic markets and government stimulation. Less formal and objective orientated but

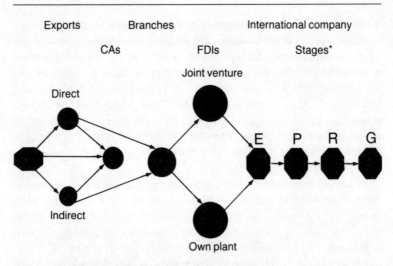

Figure 3.1 Sequential internationalization process
Source: Adapted from Hutton (1988)
Note: CAs = contractual agreements: patents, turnkey operations, licences etc.
*See Table 3.4

innovation-orientated adoption (Simpson and Kujawa 1974; Lee and Brasch 1978).

Research (Tesar and Tarleton 1982; Joynt 1982; Brookes and Rosson 1982) has shown that, in the main, the initial decision is a function of both proactive and reactive stimuli, but that factors within each have a different rank/order across research studies. The only consistent factor is an external one – the unsolicited order from a foreign customer (Simmonds and Smith 1968; Tesar 1975; Welch and Wiedersheim-Paul 1980). As Ford and Leonidou (1991) acknowledge: 'This is the first indication in the literature of the recognition of the active customer.' The existence or emergence of export stimuli is a necessary but not sufficient condition for an organization to go international. The action itself depends upon various facilitators and inhibitors surrounding the organization's history and current social structures. These are illustrated in Table 3.3. However, much of the research relating to Table 3.3 is, according to Ford and Leonidou (1991), seriously flawed. The studies suffer from linguistic, conceptual, methodological and statistical problems in their empirical testing. But poor testing should not be allowed to deny the theoretical importance of an initialization

Table 3.3 Facilitators and inhibitors to the export initiation decision

Decision-maker's characteristics
- Level of foreign market orientation
- Type and level of education
- Ethnic origin
- Ability to speak foreign languages
- Management quality and dynamism
- Perception of risk in export markets
- Perception of profits in export markets
- Perception of costs in export markets

Firm's characteristics
- Available staff time
- Paperwork and management of export operations
- Type of product line
- History of the firm
- Previous extra-regional expansion

Firm's environment characteristics
- Rules and regulations of foreign governments
- Information needed to analyse foreign markets
- Size of the domestic market
- Various infrastructural and institutional factors

Source: Adapted from Ford and Leonidou (1991)

process consisting of export stimuli amid facilitating and inhibiting factors that forms the basis of the internationalization decision.

The internationalization process that follows this initial decision is incremental/sequential (Johanson and Wiedersheim-Paul 1975; Bilkey and Tesar 1977; Cavusgil and Nevin 1980; Cavusgil 1982). This can be thought of as a learning sequence; an attempt to overcome the information, language, culture, education, business practice and legislation, that constitutes for many organizations a 'psychic distance' (Johanson and Vahlne 1977) from strange foreign markets. Cautious, incremental development helps overcome any lack of experiential knowledge or market information that otherwise create an uncertainty strong enough to prevent international development.

The remainder of the chain in Figure 3.1 continues to illustrate the incremental nature of the process. After exporting, organizations may move on to licensing (although this could be a separate, independent route) or to the setting up of sales agencies, offices or branches. As confidence in conducting international business

Table 3.4 Structures for internationalization

1 Ethnocentric
Focused on the home-country. Home country nationals are considered superior in skill and performance to foreigners either at head office or in the subsidiaries. Performance criteria and decision rules are usually based on home-country standards and there is great resistance to any change.

2 Polycentric
The opposite of ethnocentrism. The assumption is that local people know what is best and can inform organizational strategy. Subsidiaries should be as local in identity and behaviour as possible. Structurally, a polycentric organization is similar to a loose confederation of quasi-independent subsidiaries.

3 Regiocentric
Managers are recruited, developed and assigned on a regional basis. An example would be an organizational structure which lumps together operations concentrating in European countries. The assumption underlying this approach is that greater economies of scale can be achieved than with a polycentric approach, but without resorting to the more centralized focus of an ethnocentric perspective.

4 Geocentric
Both head office and local subsidiaries see themselves as important parts of the global organizational entity. Such a worldwide approach considers subsidiaries neither as satellites nor as independent operations. Managerial efforts are directed towards increasing collaboration among subsidiaries and head office to establish universal standards as well as permissible local variations.

Note: See also Figure 3.1.

increases, the decision to invest in foreign production facilities either jointly or solely may follow. Movement through these stages forces organizations to experience different structural and cultural changes. Descriptions of some of these are illustrated in Table 3.4.

Such incremental models have a proven pedagogic utility and undergo continuous development from the results of empirical research – especially in the international marketing literature. However, they have a number of shortcomings. First, the stages approach (both in exporting and in the remainder of the chain), do not explain the dynamics of progress from one stage to the next (Ford *et al.* 1982). This is aggravated by the fact that the stage boundaries lack precise definitions. Second, the unidirectional flow may, empirically, be over simplistic. In fact, the model in its illus-trated form denies divestment or strategic re-orientations surrounding a withdrawal from foreign markets. These could be due to economic recession at home or abroad, the breakdown of trust/confidence in agents or licensees, the expropriation of FDI production assets or economical or political instability (e.g. the phased withdrawal of European assets from South Africa in the mid to late 1980s). Moreover, recent research on MNCs operating in Venezuela (Jatar 1992) reveals that certain large MNCs had to open up final markets themselves (e.g. in beer) where entrepreneurs had yet to establish their own facilities. After aiding this establishment through grants and assets, the MNCs withdrew to the production stage.

Third, the sequential nature of the process essentially denies the leapfrogging of stages, e.g. from exporting straight to FDI or straight to FDI (via acquisition) from a mainly domestic base. The latter course being symptomatic of much recent internationalization in Europe prior to the establishment of the world's largest single market in 1992. Fourth, they have been adversely criticized for representing a process of great complexity in too simple a format (Dichtl *et al.* 1983). Fifthly, their unidirectionality assumes or at least suggests a cause and effect relationship. The complexity of the process coupled with the possibility of feedback loops representing re-orientations aggravates the interpretation of the ordering of the variables. Consequently, empirical testing in the area is fraught with difficulty. This may only be resolved by longitudinal studies which are rare and expensive. Finally, explanations of the choices available to the organizations at any point in time are not made clear. Sugges-tions are made that FDI may be superior to licensing where trans-action costs of the latter are higher, where organizational advantages lie in a continuous flow of innovative knowledge and where indige-nous technological advantages are coupled with an excess of capacity of capital and managerial skills. But these broad, general statements are the results of a concentration of research on the FDI stage rather than on the whole process. Hence they are, at best, only partial suggestions.

But the existence of the single unidirectional, sequential process may be easily explained. Europe has had a strong tradition of research into international business. The geographic dispersion and size of its many nation states, means that this research has concen-trated on internationalization from a single country base. Indeed, many European companies, up to the late 1970s, were essentially international rather than multinational – a fact that may have constrained the nature of the research process and its outcomes. Even during the 1980s and into the 1990s, many British-based multinationals were still Anglo-Saxon in the spread of their operations – many of which were tightly controlled from British bases.

Hence, the development and utility of the sequential model may well be restricted in its applicability to a specific location and during a specific time. The emergence of industrialization in LDCs and DCs has occurred in a different era of international business, one in which the infrastructures for such trade are better developed. The Taiwanese companies can now move directly from OEM manufacturer (for exports) straight to FDI by acquisition – these examples were noted earlier in the chapter. Stage models may no longer provide appropriate explanations of all internationalization processes in the modern era. However, an individual focus upon each stage may still provide some utility and direction.

Competing theories of modern times have focused on the FDI stage, especially the horizontal variety (same product as the domestic market) as opposed to vertical (addition of a stage of production) or conglomerate (different products from the domestic market) types. Theoretically, in all of these cases, there must be a host of competing reasons why organizations invest in direct facilities abroad. In reality, what are the most important?

At bottom, the answer can be an easy one. Organizations are bundles of assets and their contemporary worth is judged by the present value of their future cash flows, adjusted by a rate that reflects the associated risk of those flows. Following traditional finance theory, maximizing the worth amounts to either increasing revenues, decreasing costs and/or decreasing the risk of the revenue flows. Clearly, organizations pursue domestic and foreign investments with these three methods in mind:

- *Increase returns*: by capitalizing on specific advantages and/or imperfections in target markets, e.g. by exploiting a patent protection internationally.
- *Decreasing costs*: by improving the efficiency of operations in the value chain, e.g. by locating where factors of production are cheapest.
- *Decreasing risks*: by diversifying the asset base, e.g. by locating in a balanced spread of international locations where economic peaks and troughs occur at different times.

Generally, the competing modern theories of FDI address one or more of these fundamental cash-flow issues. The following discussion will concentrate on the more prominent approaches and theories.

Market imperfection theories

Structural imperfections

By 1960, neo-classical financial theory with its restrictive assumptions of perfect competition, zero transaction costs and interest-rate differentials as the sole drivers of capital movements was still the most accepted explanation of international capital flows. As we have witnessed, both world trade and FDIs increased dramatically since the mid 1950s, yet there was no separate theory of FDIs. In 1960, Stephen Hymer produced a seminal doctoral dissertation that broke the intellectual straitjacket imposed by neo-classical theory. Dunning and Rugman (1985) emphasize the gravity of Hymer's breakthrough: 'the pioneering conceptual insight of Hymer was to break out of the arid mould of international trade and investment theory and focus attention on the Multi-National Enterprise per se.' Up to this point, it was not possible under the trade and investment theories examined so far, to explain why multi-nationals transfer intermediate products (knowledge or technology) across international boundaries whilst retaining control of them.

Hymer's theory relies heavily on the previous work at Harvard University of Joe Bain (1956: see Chapter 1) on the structural characteristics of markets and industries. Essentially, an organization must possess a sufficient specific advantage to overcome its fear (e.g. language, culture, geographic distance etc.) or lack of knowledge of foreign markets. This advantage must[8] be sufficiently great to outweigh the presumed asset-based advantage of nationally located organizations to induce foreign investment to occur. These specific advantages rely on barriers to entry for protection and sustenance. Caves (1982) asserts that the most powerful source of specific advantage is product differentiation through, for example, patented differentiated product or production methods (technological) or marketing investments in branding, styling, distribution and service. However, other sources are significant in fostering a competitive advantage such as economies of scale, access to capital, multi-plant economies and excess resources (e.g. managerial skills and liquid reserves).

Structural market imperfections enable organizations to utilize the power given by their specific advantage to close markets and obtain superior rents on their activities. In Hymer's words MNEs exist for monopolistic reasons: 'to separate markets and prevent competition between units'. On the contrary, if production factor and output markets were efficient, organizations would not be able to sustain monopolistic advantages and, arguably, the amount of FDI would be much reduced.

Clearly the influential writings of Porter (1980; 1985) twenty years later on strategic management, which emphasized the role of building generic strategies on sustainable competitive advantages behind entry and exit barriers, can be directly linked to the original work of Hymer, and both works can be traced to Bain.[9]

Such conditions and consequent advantages are typical of oligopolistic markets. Organizations in oligopolies with the same kind of product (e.g. timber) tend to be responsible for vertical-type FDIs while oligopolists with differentiated products are generally responsible for horizontal-type FDIs. A differentiated advantage behind high entry barriers in domestic markets means the control of an asset, usually knowledge, that can be efficiently transferred to foreign markets (Caves 1971).

Dunning and Rugman (1985) note two further important attributes of Hymer's work. First, the emphasis on market structure and the dynamic nature of the specific advantage of MNEs fits in well with the PLC models of Vernon and the nature of competitive reactions to innovations. Any advantage for a single MNE is continuously threatened by competitors who launch new products, gain new technology and so new specific advantages accrue to them. Vernon's model, besides being a theory of trade is also clearly a theory of FDI, spelling out the stages when organizations will use their specific advantages to invest abroad. Vernon's PLC is the clearest link between the theories of trade and investment but rests, like Hymer's theory, upon a specific advantage that can be bid away over time by rivals. Second, Hymer states that: 'profits in one country may be negatively correlated with profits of another country ... an investor may be able to achieve greater stability in his profitability by diversifying his portfolio and investing part in each country'.

Hence, Hymer recognized diversification as a main motivating force enabling risk spreading in either individual or corporate port-folios. The latter is of particular importance where costs of carrying out the transactions internationally for individuals are greater than those for organizations. In modern strategic management, companies balance their portfolios of strategic business units inter-nationally to reduce the risk component of their returns by investing in economies at different stages of the business cycles, ultimately to prevent over exposure to recessions. This insight by Hymer is even more remarkable given that the modern theory of finance incorpor-ating asset-pricing models and the mean-variance framework of returns was yet to be fully developed in 1960, when he submitted his doctoral thesis.

However, a few problems remain. First, Hymer's comparison of internationalization with 'contractual collusion' among oligopolists and the rooting of the theory in the exploitation of market imper-fections through monopolistic advantage led to an unfortunate rationale for the regulation of MNEs. Subsequently they were seen by some nation states as unsavoury rogues. Second, Hymer neglected the geographic and spatial dimensions of international-ization going some way to explaining why FDI occurs, but not where. Our previous discussion of comparative-cost advantage underlies the important nature of location for MNEs attempting to improve operational efficiency, thereby increasing cash flows by reducing costs. Finally, Hymer's theory does not explain why FDI is the only route to foreign market operations. High tariff barriers, transport costs, government inducements and the need for close proximity to local markets are sound enough reasons for foreign market management of assets. But why should the investing company undertake this task itself?

Indeed, it could sell the asset to an indigenous firm that is more familiar with local market conditions, e.g. by licensing. There must be other crucial market imperfections other than structural ones that prevent it from so doing. In particular, these imperfections may relate to transaction costs, that arise external to the organization. These external market imperfections may lead the MNE to develop an internal market (through FDI) as a substitute for either the lack of an external market for goods and services (e.g. in the pricing of knowledge) or to replace more expensive modes of transaction. Clearly, in these circumstances the MNE is acting to increase efficiency due to market imperfections and few, if any, monopolistic rents will accrue. This view is opposed to the one denoting exploitation of a specific advantage in response to market imperfections where monopolistic rents are far more likely to accrue. It is a matter of efficiency gains versus exploitation.

Transaction costs

Supporters of the transaction-costs approach to the explanation of FDI (Teece 1981; Rugman 1981; Hennart 1982; Dunning 1981; Buckley and Casson 1976) rely on the path breaking works of Coase (1937) and Williamson (1975) on market imperfections and trans-action costs. The standpoint of a firm-specific advantage is the same as under the structural imperfections theory above. Similarly, it is the possession of this advantage that enables organizations to over-come the perceived advantages of local firms and hence induces them to enter foreign markets. If the specific advantage is knowledge-based (e.g. technological) that represents a cumulative experience in R&D, the problem becomes complex. Organizations could choose to license the know-how (e.g. as Pilkington's, UK, did with its technologically advanced float-glass process). But, as knowledge is a public good, any advantage quickly dissipates upon exploitation. How does an organization provide sufficient inform-ation on such an asset without revealing the asset itself? The buyer will be more uncertain than the seller of its value, hence the market for intangible assets tends to fail. This forces organizations to exploit the inherent asset value by retaining control over its management. This can apply domestically or internationally. If trade barriers, government inducements, transaction costs and factory costs favour international expansion, organizations will then enter the market themselves by direct investment. Underlying this approach is the crucial assumption that the internal market is more efficient than the external one for the intangible asset. In these circumstances, Hennart (1982) argues that FDI can be expected to be more frequent among technologically intensive companies, intent on sheltering trade secrets.

This internalization approach has many merits. It examines the very nature of exchange relationships. These would be easy in perfect markets where humans were both honest and had full information. In reality, costs are incurred in such transactions, e.g. information, bargaining and costs of enforcing the contract. More-over, such exchange is often limited by the inability of individuals or management teams to absorb all knowledge (bounded rationality) in the decision-making process, by the opportunism of individuals (their ability to cheat) and the nature of the asset under consideration (e.g. does it have an alternative use?). Williamson (1975) has argued, theoretically, that all three of the latter limitations must be present if organizations are to efficiently replace external markets by internalization within their own hierarchy. Rugman (1986) has shown that all these limitations can be circumvented within MNEs. For instance, the use of environmental scanning and management information systems would help to overcome the limitations of bounded rationality.

Moreover, the internalization approach can help organizations select between modes of entry in the internationalization process, e.g. between exporting, licensing and FDI, provided that extra conditions are included in the approach. For example, the choice between licensing and FDI depends on factors such as the risk of knowledge dissipation, enforcement costs, the state of proprietary technology in the PLC, probabilities of substitute products and so on. Similarly, the choice between exports and FDI will be influenced by information on changes in tariff and non-tariff barriers. This almost forces internalization into a firm-level, strategic decision-making model. So, if there is a low risk of dissipation, licensing may be preferred over FDI; if tariff barriers are low, exports may be preferred over licensing and FDI. The final decision on entry mode will depend on the governance costs associated with each entry mode. For instance, Teece (1985) argues that the governance costs of licensing are increased by many types of contracting costs, including opportunism, the specific nature of the asset and asymmetries of information. In these circumstances, it makes sense for the organization to substitute internal markets (FDI) for licensing or for export, if the latter is ruled out for either transportational or factor-cost disadvantages.

However, the approach is not without its critics. In the main, these focus on whether internalization is a general and predictive theory. Buckley (1983) argues that it is a 'concept in search of a theory'. It is tautological, as firms automatically internalize imperfect markets until the cost of so doing outweighs any benefits. Casson (1982) argues that 'internalization is in fact a general theory of why firms exist'. Kay (1983) states that 'internalization does not satisfy the condition of refutability that is required for theory'. But even as an approach, rather than a theory, Rugman (1986) argues for its strong predictive power which explains when organizations will or will not internalize markets. This, in itself, is a major contribution to the FDI debate.

Limitations of FDI approaches and theories

The explanations of direct investment discussed so far (PLC, structural and transaction imperfections) are all based on a specific advantage; the possession of which leads to direct international investment by overcoming organizations' fears of foreign markets and the perceived advantages of local firms. In the introduction, the dramatic growth of foreign investments by Swedish companies in the EC was illustrated.

A high proportion of these foreign investments are in countries with which they have long been familiar and know how to do business. These developments call into question the explanatory power of the modern approaches to FDI. Just as the rapidly changing pattern of world trade and FDI had surpassed the predictive and explanatory capabilities of classical trade and investment theories, the modern theories may just be children of their time, incapable of explaining contemporary developments in international business. They have a number of important limitations.

First, the possession of a specific advantage as a driver for FDI may be appropriate for firms seeking to internationalize for the first time. Their fear of foreign markets and the perceived advantages of local firms may both be overcome by the size of the inherent specific advantage. This provides a credible explanation of the decision to own and operate subsidiaries in foreign markets. However, it does not provide a sufficiently convincing explanation for the activities of experienced international firms with a large proportion of their total assets abroad. Forsgren (1989) argues that the driving force behind reinvestments, aimed at keeping subsidiaries in good shape, and behind new investments may well be instigated by the experienced foreign assets themselves. Many contemporary multinational companies are highly experienced and have invested abroad in familiar markets to such an extent that any disadvantages due to fear have long since disappeared and the need for any specific advantage with which to pursue other FDIs is therefore called into question.

Second, in many of the recent cases of FDI in Europe and North America the mode of entry has been by acquisition. The crucial assumption of a firm's specific advantage is far more difficult to propose as an explanation of this current trend. Certainly, control or management of the specific advantage is difficult to maintain within an acquisition process, rendering much of the internalization argument inappropriate. This shortcoming of the internalization approach has been admitted by one of its major proposers (Rugman 1982). Acquisition is a quick route to internationalization and such takeovers also enable predators to remain competitive by acquiring other firms' specific advantages. For instance, 70 per cent of Tube Investment's (UK) growth in the late 1980s was through a foreign-acquisition programme which broadened its international spread of activities in specialized engineering. Furthermore, the acquisitive experiences of Forsgren's Swedish cases, e.g. PLM (glass packaging) and Electrolux (domestic appliances) in Europe also fortify this assertion. Hence, a domestic specific advantage is not necessarily that important if the internationalization process develops through acquisition.

Finally, conventional approaches and theories rarely distinguish between the types of FDIs that occur. For experienced companies, the twenty-fifth FDI is the result of a process that incorporates replacement investments, minor expansions, new subsidiaries and acquisitions. The first FDI may well have been a result of the firm's attempts to internalize a market, but the later investment decisions would, as Forsgren (1989) stresses, be the result of many other considerations with internalization taking a minor role. In fact, in his study of 25 of Sweden's largest foreign investors between 1975 and 1982, 81 per cent of FDIs were either replacements or minor expansions to maintain and develop the capacity of already existing production plants and market organizations. In addition, over 85 per cent of new investments were by acquisition.

This sample is specific to Swedish companies who, by tradition, are at the vanguard of the internationalization process, due to the small size of their domestic markets. But as we have seen in the case of Taiwan, the trend of internationalization by acquisition is a real one. Modern theoretical approaches to FDI require either a major development (or even replacement) if they are to explain these recent empirical trends.

NETWORK THEORY

Theories explaining the FDI decision may have to move into a new, perhaps 'post-modernist', era to explain the prevailing empirical evidence. A useful starting point builds upon the previously mentioned Swedish research by Forsgren (1989).[10] In his examination of the recent internationalization patterns of Swedish companies, the evidence rejects the traditional approaches that lead to FDI by way of exports, licensing branches, and the wholly owned subsidiary. This successive-stage strategy reflected the conventional mode of internationalization for many organizations, particularly in the 1960s and 1970s and the many previous empirical studies of the Uppsala School bear this out (Johansen and Wiedersheim-Paul 1974; Forsgren and Johansen 1975; Johansen and Vahlne 1977). It reflects the fear/uncertainty argument that organizations have of foreign markets and so ties in well with the market imperfection theories. As we have seen, recent 'instantaneous' international entry modes have come through acquisition and this practice is commonplace in both the advanced industrial nations as well as the LDCs.

Moreover, the successive-stages model supports a centre-periphery perspective of organizational structures (i.e. the parent company based in its domestic home land decides upon and implements international expansion decisions). The strategic decision making is essentially hierarchical. However, with the recent growth in acquisitions, coupled with the long experience of internationalization by many organizations, the majority of their assets may not be on domestic shores. This development leads logically to a centre-centre perspective of the organization, i.e. that decisions to internationalize may no longer come from the centre but from well established and experienced foreign subsidiaries.[11]

To understand strategic decisions in the 'centre-centre' structure, perspectives must shift from the rational, hierarchic to the viewing of the organization as a coalition of interests after Cyert and March (1963: see Chapter 1) and Pfeffer (1978). An experienced, widely spread, international organization is an interdependent system embracing both competing and dependent interests. Hence, strategic decision making and international expansion affects the whole corporate network and is not just a headquarters/foreign-subsidiary issue.

There are two competing perspectives of strategy formation. It is either rationally formed and intended or it emerges (Mintzberg 1988). The rational process is at the heart of all FDI approaches. But, as Forsgren (1989) argues: 'Foreign investment behaviour should perhaps be described instead as a pattern in a stream of activities which becomes apparent after a while and which is then described by top management as corporate strategy.' This relatively

new perspective has enabled him to classify the approaches to international business (Figure 3.2). It is in the 'politically' orientated
literature that better explanations of the recent empirical evidence in
internationalization may be found, e.g. growth through acquisitions.
One explanation lies in network theory.

The premises of network theory are as follows:

1   Organizations are related to a network of other organizations
    and to understand individual organizational behaviour it is
    necessary to understand these relationships.
2   Organizations are dependent on other organizations for
    resources and this ties them together based upon reciprocal
    transactions.

Strategic behaviour as:	International firm as:	
	Hierarchy	Coalition of interests
Rational planning	Conventional theories of FDI [See pp. 90–103]	Political power of subsidiaries
Pattern of activities	Sequential stage process of internationalization [See Figure 3.1]	Political view of complex organizations in internationalization e.g. networks [See Figure 3.4]

Figure 3.2 Four views of the internationalization process
Source: Based on the work of Forsgren (1989)

3   Resources controlled by individual organizations are all different and not comparable; hence investments are made in the relationships between them that create value in their dependent linkages. Productive and marketing capacities of organizations are adjusted to match those of others in the network by an investment in physical and human assets which reinforces the bonding of the industrial network.

4   The network is in constant flux as suppliers, buyers and customers may enter and exit.

5   The strength of the individual organization depends, not on specific advantages as in the market-imperfection theories but on links with customers, suppliers, distributors, competitors and so on.

6   Research evidence (Hallen *et al.* 1987) has shown that information exchange and adaptation processes are key attributes of the networks.

7   The character of the products of exchange influences the extent of the bonding in the network, e.g. hi-tech products require much closer liaison between organizations (e.g. Silicon Glen in Scotland, Silicon Valley in California).

Indeed, some writers have argued (e.g. Miles and Snow 1986) that the network form is especially pertinent to markets characterized by sophisticated and rapidly changing technology exposed to the continuous shift in international trade and competition. Here, traditional organizational structures have failed to cope and the network has emerged as a superior form of organizational design. This very prescriptive view of networks contrasts with the alternative, descriptive, view in the literature. In the latter, the network is used as an 'analytical convenience' (Cunningham and Culligan 1991) for understanding industrial systems. This approach allows the application of network concepts – power, dependency, trust, exchange, money, information and utilities (that flow along the links in the network) – to the analysis of corporate behaviour: 'For the understanding of the configuration of any particular network, the flows of power and information may actually be more important than those of money and utilities' Thorelli (1986).

Entire networks are founded as information utilities (e.g. airlines, travel agents and captive computer reservations systems). The market for online information services (OIS) is one example of these competence-enhancing relationships. The four basic competencies necessary for the provision of an OIS – database supply, data processing, software supply and telecommunications – are illustrated in Figure 3.3. The different players have different roles relating to their areas of competence above, but as a whole, they link up in a network of value added to offer an OIS to the market.

Typical strategic issues resolved in a networking context include:

- Corporate positioning.
- Product positioning.
- Market channels and franchising.
- Turnkey contracts and systems selling.
- Barter and reciprocal trading.
- Split vs unified sourcing.
- Cartels.

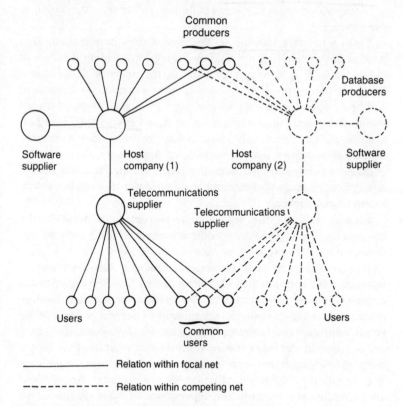

Figure 3.3 Networks in online information services
Source: Cunningham and Culligan (1991)

- Interlocking directorates.
- Diversification and vertical integration.
- Joint ventures, mergers and acquisitions.
- Internationalization.

As can be seen, the network idea is particularly applicable in international business and industrial and international marketing. This explains why much of the empirical research has come from marketeers working on customer–supplier relationships in an international context (Hakansson 1982; Mattsson 1986; Cunningham and Culligan 1991; Forsstrom 1991; Easton and Lundgren 1991). Furthermore, at first sight the emphasis may be seen to be on cooperation. But the underlying motivation is still the notion of gaining a competitive advantage. Hence, strong intra-net and extra-net competition exists that ensures fluidity rather than stagnation in the network.

 From a network standpoint, the view of the internationalization process begins to change. First, any strategic investment is meant to obtain, defend or develop a position in the network. If an organization is already involved in a foreign network, its direct investment will be to defend or develop its position; if it is not, its direct investment will be to obtain a position within it. In network theory, organizations do not necessarily invest solely to build upon a specific advantage as argued in the conventional approaches above but, for experienced international organizations, the investments are to strengthen, manage and monitor their positions in already existing international networks.

 Second, because the organization is part of a network, the importance of any company-specific advantage is much reduced. An organization's strength does not solely depend on a specific advantage but more upon its network linkages. Any asset-specific advantage is constrained by the network in which the organization operates. Hence, from an internationalization perspective, foreign-entry mode depends upon the organization's current position in the chain from exports, licensing, branches, wholly-owned subsidiary *and* acquisition. Network theory suggests that organizations have a range of bridging strategies to manage these linkages in the network (e.g. negotiation, contracts, alliances or acquisitions). Acquisitions are therefore used to handle the dependence on other organizations.

For the internationalization process, there is an important distinction to be made. If foreign networks are new to the organization, acquisition is probably too big a step. It may be better to maintain the existing network (e.g. of suppliers) by entering foreign markets by direct investment in own-plant and equipment. This retention of the existing framework (or recipe) or way of doing business (see Chapter 2) provides a level of certainty and stability which may overcome any fear of a foreign market. Acquisitions at this stage would mean taking over an existing organization with its already well-developed network. This may be too much to handle for the new internationalist. However, with the experienced internationalist, who is developing and defending the network position, the more likely that acquisitions will be used as bridging strategies, until they come to dominate foreign-investment decisions. Hence, investments in own facilities will precede acquisitions in the internationalization process.

Network theory predicts that as the degree of internationalization gets larger then the number of acquisitions will follow suit – the opposite result to internalization theory which has a problem in coping with the acquisitive process. As Forsgren (1989) states: 'This contradiction results from the fact that internalization theory stresses the difficulty adherent in the ignorance of foreign markets while network theory emphasizes the problem of moving the intangible asset without moving "its roots".'

In this chapter so far, we have closely examined the competing theories explaining international trade and investment. In particular, we noted how conventional economic approaches to FDI (market imperfection and transaction costs theories) failed to cope fully with the observed recent trends towards internationalization through acquisitions. Network theory provides a partial explanation of these events.

For the practitioner, it is important to be able to operationalize the rich knowledge contained within these theories. To meet this requirement, we have included two summary tables (3.5 and 3.6) that will help to bring much of this section together. Moreover, the next section is orientated around developing a suitable, practical, international strategy. It provides techniques, underpinned by much of the theory discussed so far, to facilitate the international decision by couching the analysis and selection firmly in pragmatic terms.

BLENDING THEORY AND PRACTICE

The competing trade and investment theories encountered in this chapter provide a powerful basis for understanding the dynamic

Table 3.5 Operational theories of internationalization

Theory	Strategic ideas
Trade	
• Mercantilism	Maximize exports over imports and use surplus to fortify position.
• Classical theory	Maximize goods and services through trade, which occurs because countries have cost differences in production.
• Extensions (Hecksher-Ohlin)	Source of comparative advantage between nations is based upon a ratio of labour to those of land and capital.
Trade and investment	
Product life cycle	Products start and gain critical mass in advanced nations and internationalization follows through exports to FDI and, on maturity, production is almost wholly located in LDCs.
Investment	
• Stage models	Empiricism shows internationalization begins through an initial decision influenced by inhibiting and facilitating stimuli and follows an incremental process from exports to contractual agreements to branches to FDI. Consistent with PLC above. Provides understanding but few choices.
• Structural imperfections	Specific advantage at root of any international expansion; if possessed, organizations can seek out market imperfections, close markets and obtain superior rents. Consistent with PLC and stage models above. Provides explanations but few choices.
• Transaction costs	Specific advantage still at root, consistent with SI theory above. Where the transaction costs of an administrative exchange are lower than a market exchange, organizations will internalize markets. Hence, in international

terms, if trade barriers, government inducements, transaction costs and factory costs favour international expansion, organizations will exploit intangible assets (e.g. technology) by foreign direct investments. Provides selection criteria for FDI choice over exports and licensing.

- Network theory
No specific advantage necessary at the organizational level unlike the SI and TC theories above. This is assumed to be possessed by the network as a whole, that together provides a value added product or a service to the market.

Provides selection criteria for FDI choice over acquisitions.

Table 3.6 Control, resources and risk through internationalization

	Exports	Licensing	JVs	FDI	Acquisitions
Control	High	Low	Med	High	Medium
Resources	Medium	Low	Med	High	High
Risk	Low	High	Med	Low	Low

Note: The three variables indicate the level of control retained through ownership, the extent of resource commitment (especially managerial) and the risk attached to losing a specific advantage in know-how (e.g. technology, marketing) that could be expropriated by a licensee or a joint-venture partner.

elements of the internationalization of organizations. The summary table at the end of the last section helps to synthesize the material and goes some way to prescribing operational choices and steps in what has been established to be quite a difficult ground to interpret. To further assist managers in making pragmatic choices, a variety of decision-making techniques have been developed by economists working in the international business field: (see Porter's configuration/co-ordination grid 1986; globalization, Tinsley 1986; challenge of European 1992 markets, Friberg 1988). Two of the more practical are now described in the hope that they could help managers put together all the material that has been received so far.

The two techniques that are presented are based upon the development of portfolio-like matrices. Hence, all the reservations concerning difficulties and dangers in their construction and use must be emphasized once again (see Chapter 1).

PRAGMATIC GUIDES

Solberg's strategic windows

Solberg's basic premise is that the leaner and more flexible organizations of small and medium-sized enterprises (SMEs) seem to better facilitate the free flow of information and to foster more proactive attitudes to internationalization that overcome many 'psychic distances'. He had found (Solberg 1988) that SMEs in Norway were more successful at exporting than their larger counterparts (the greater tendency of smaller nations to look beyond their borders is an obvious factor to consider in interpreting his work). Subsequently, he developed a comprehensive framework, aimed at addressing the challenge created by globalization, given the unique aspects of SMEs. Figure 3.4 illustrates his nine strategic windows.

The framework is built around two dimensions, one internal (company preparedness for internationalization: CPI), and one external (degree of globality of the industry: DGI). Notice that the dimensions are segmented simply along qualitative bases – of high/ moderate/low for CPI on the vertical axis and local, potential and global for DGI on the horizontal axis. Each scale contains objectively measured criteria (e.g. international sales) but there is always the potential to develop the dimensions by the incorporation of other aspects, for example more qualitative and heuristically based ones, that are better suited to specific organizational circumstances. This reflects the approach of the GE business screen that was presented in Chapter 1. The guidelines for the incorporation of criteria into each dimension are given below:

Company preparedness for internationalization

Corporate culture

The percentage of total sales in the international markets is, for example, a proxy for how 'international' the business is at present.

Company preparedness for internationalization	Degree of globality of the industry		
	Local	Potentially global	global
High	Enter new business	Prepare for globalization	Strengthen global position
Moderate	Consolidate export markets	Expand in international markets	Seek alliances and global niches
Low	Stay at home	Develop international niches	Prepare for a buy-out

Figure 3.4 Solberg's nine strategic windows
Source: Solberg (1989)

Relative market share in major markets

This relates to the reference market in which customers *perceive* the marketeers products to lie, i.e. where competition actually takes place.

Globality of the industry

Supplier structure and potential development

This is measured by two factors – competitive structure and national specialization.

Competitive structure

This relates to the number and size of competitors, economies of scale etc. (Porter's value chain and industry analysis (1980; 1985) can be readily used as a preliminary analysis.)

National specialization

- *National industry*: dominated by national suppliers or a fragmented competitive structure.
- *Regional industry*: domestic suppliers are involved in exporting and MNCs have made some inroads. International trade is important but no dominant players, e.g. furniture, clothing and building materials.
- *Global industry*: presence of a limited number of global, dominating suppliers, e.g. aircraft industry with Boeing, McDonnell-Douglas and Airbus.

Market accessibility

This relates to trade barriers, government shelter strategies (see Rugman and Verbeke, 1991), complexity of distribution channel systems (e.g. Japan), customs, transport costs etc.

Combining the international preparedness of the company with the globality of the industry enables strategic options to be assessed. The windows delineate the major strategic focus of top management. Once again, the technique is a first-phase approach to internationalization and applies, in particular, to SMEs. However, the generic extensions beyond exporting, e.g. alliances, globalization etc., can apply to existing international organizations. Moreover, the technique allows for internationalization by acquisition (develop international niches, expand in international markets) and consequently allows for the building of networks.

On the down side, the technique suffers from all the usual impediments of matrix analytical forms (see Chapter 1). In particular, the reduction of a complex process to two dimensions may be too simple given that risk and uncertainty are not explicitly dealt with, but subsumed within the dimension components. Furthermore, tasks pertaining to technology, marketing, human resource management and financial aspects are not captured. Overall, the technique is useful in providing a first-phase introduction to the area by stimulating international thinking – perhaps for the first time, and also helps to summarize for the practitioner many of the complicated, theoretical arguments that have underpinned its design.

Country portfolio analysis

Portfolio techniques are aimed at assisting organizations to get a balance of age, financial, sectoral, and international elements in their businesses or products. Multinational companies have long been avid users of portfolios to assess the international balance of their businesses – by 1982 over 45 per cent of them were using this facility (Haspeslagh 1982). These techniques have two main uses: the positioning of SBUs and country portfolio analysis.

Positioning of strategic business units

This example (see Figure 3.5) illustrates Norton's business unit spread across the countries that it serves. The technique aids managers in balancing the conflicting positions of businesses, some of which may be stars in the UK but cash cows in Nigeria, dogs in France and yet question marks in India. In the Norton case, the businesses, although strong in most countries, are focused on low-growth/low-share positions. This may be too conservative a profile, too low risk. High growth rates, although coupled with greater risk, may help open up and establish a major presence in other markets.

Country portfolio analysis

To help assess the risk and economic potential of countries that organizations are contemplating entrance to, economists have developed portfolio models. The portfolios that follow have been developed by Perlitz (1985). They are illustrated in Figure 3.6. They deliberately mirror the growth share matrix (see Chapter 1) in the identification and use of variables that reflect market growth and market share – or more broadly, competitive position. Hence, for market growth, they substitute the average growth rate of gross domestic product (say over a 5-year period), which is an important indicator for the market opportunities of a specific country. Low GDP growth rates may reflect stagnating or saturated markets or even a lack of factor endowments (e.g. capital). For market share, as

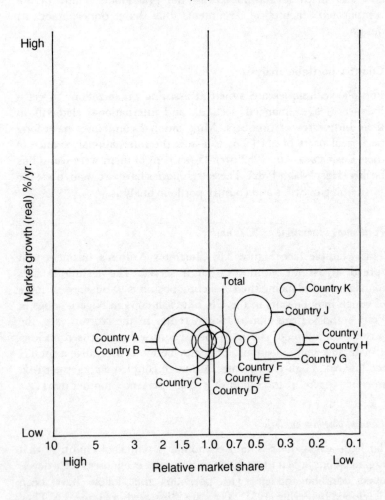

Region D – business g – by country
balloon areas proportional to sales

Figure 3.5 Positioning of strategic business units

Source: Robert Cushman (1979) 'Norton's top-down, bottom-up planning process', pp. 6–7

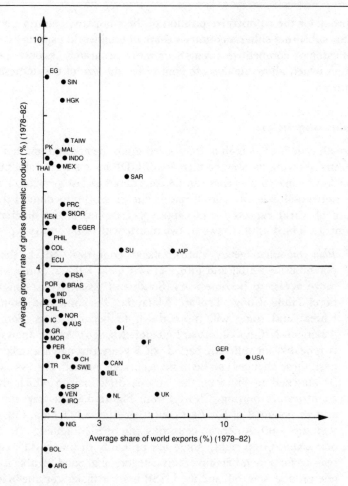

Figure 3.6 Country portfolio matrix

Source: Perlitz (1985)

Notes: ARG = Argentina, AUS = Australia, BEL = Belgium, BOL = Bolivia, BRAS = Brazil, CAN = Canada, CH = Switzerland, CHIL = Chile, COL = Colombia, DK = Denmark, ECU = Ecuador, EG = Egypt, EGER = East Germany, ESP = Spain, F = France, GER = West Germany, GR = Greece, HGK = Hong Kong, I = Italy, IC = Ivory Coast, IND = India, INDO = Indonesia, IRL = Ireland, IRQ = Iraq, ISR = Israel, JAP = Japan, KEN = Kenya, MAL = Malaysia, MEX = Mexico, MOR = Morocco, NIG = Nigeria, NL = The Netherlands, NOR = Norway, PER = Peru, PHIL = The Philippines, PK = Pakistan, POR = Portugal, PRC = People's Republic of China, RSA = Republic of South Africa, SAR = Saudi Arabia, SIN = Singapore, SKOR = South Korea, SU = Soviet Union, SWE = Sweden, TAIW = Taiwan, THAI = Thailand, TR = Turkey, UK = United Kingdom, USA = United States of America, VEN = Venezuela, Z = Zaire.

a proxy for the competitive position of the company, country portfolios substitute either a country's share of total world exports as an
indicator of competitive strength or more accurately, exports per
capita which allows analysts to control for the size of the domestic
country.

Matrix interpretation

Growth is defined as high or low, based upon the assumption that a
country showing an average increase of GDP in real terms of 4 per
cent for 5 consecutive years can be considered as fast growing. For
the horizontal axis, the cut-off rate is chosen as the median of the
share of world exports (or of exports per capita) of the different
countries. The output is a two by two matrix with four country types:

1   *Baby countries*: newly industrialized countries: NICs: their
    potential for actual and future growth is as follows. Some will
    move across to become stars (South-east Asian NICs: Singa-
    pore, Hong Kong, Taiwan, Malaysia, Thailand and South
    Korea) and some will move down to become dogs (South
    American NICs: Columbia, Ecuador, Mexico). As the analysis
    is repeated for different periods of 5 years through the recent
    past, these changes can be more accurately plotted. Arrows can
    be attached to illustrate the various directions in which the
    countries are moving. Clearly, from Figure 3.6, the important
    growth potential of Far East countries especially China, rather
    than the South American countries, can be highlighted.
2   *Star countries* (top right): there are probably distinctly different
    reasons for a membership of this category, e.g. Saudi Arabia is a
    one-product star (oil) and the USSR is an artificial star due to its
    forced exports (e.g. weaponry) to the captive Eastern bloc
    countries during this period.
3   *Cash cow countries* (bottom right): most western industrialized
    countries (WICs) where markets have mainly matured. But
    income levels, standard of living and quality of life remain high.
    So new markets could still open up and the large critical mass of
    income still makes these economies attractive (USA, West
    Germany, Italy, France, UK, Canada).
4   *Dog countries* (bottom left): despite the condescending termin-
    ology, many countries (e.g. Australia, Norway, Switzerland,
    Sweden, Finland and Denmark) will probably stay relatively

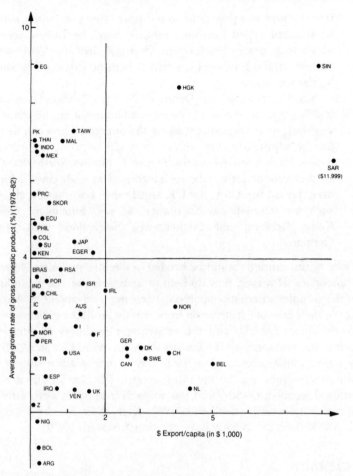

Figure 3.7 Revised country portfolio matrix

Source: Perlitz (1985)

Notes: ARG = Argentina, AUS = Australia, BEL = Belgium, BOL = Bolivia, BRAS = Brazil, CAN = Canada, CH = Switzerland, CHIL = Chile, COL = Colombia, DK = Denmark, ECU = Ecuador, EG = Egypt, EGER = East Germany, ESP = Spain, F = France, GER = West Germany, GR = Greece, HGK = Hong Kong, I = Italy, IC = Ivory Coast, IND = India, INDO = Indonesia, IRL = Ireland, IRQ = Iraq, ISR = Israel, JAP = Japan, KEN = Kenya, MAL = Malaysia, MEX = Mexico, MOR = Morocco, NIG = Nigeria, NL = The Netherlands, NOR = Norway, PER = Peru, PHIL = The Philippines, PK = Pakistan, POR = Portugal, PRC = People's Republic of China, RSA = Republic of South Africa, SAR = Saudi Arabia, SIN = Singapore, SKOR = South Korea, SU = Soviet Union, SWE = Sweden, TAIW = Taiwan, THAI = Thailand, TR = Turkey, UK = United Kingdom, USA = United States of America, VEN = Venezuela, Z = Zaire.

wealthy and prosperous for some time. However, some countries had dropped into this category from the baby category above (e.g. Brazil, Peru, Spain, Portugal, Ireland, Venezuela, Greece, India, Iraq) and concern should be expressed at their 'underdog' status.

Smaller countries (e.g. Denmark, Sweden, Norway) may find it difficult to achieve a 3 per cent median mark on the share of world exports. The variable along the horizontal axis can therefore be adjusted to cope with country size by using exports per capita. Such a revised matrix (Figure 3.7) shows clearly that the smaller economies can be re-categorized as cash cows. Moreover, Japan, the USA, the UK and France have not developed such an international orientation as say, Singapore, Hong Kong, Belgium, the Netherlands, Switzerland and West Germany.

Once again, caution should be heeded in the interpretation of these approaches. However, they do help to structure our understanding of the complex international arena. Their main advantage probably lies in their ease of construction from readily available statistics (e.g. World Bank, OECD) and the consequent readiness of interpretation. In common with the growth-share matrix in Chapter 1, they represent a first-phase approach and can be reinforced by the use of other techniques (e.g. by the introduction of bankers' estimates of political, economic and social risk in each country to form a risk/opportunity matrix – see Perlitz 1985; Kern 1985; Friedmann and Kim 1988; and for an early interpretation Stobaugh 1969).

SUMMARY

This chapter has reviewed the major theories of trade and investment in the light of recent empirical evidence that suggests the majority of internationalization in modern times is by acquisition. Conventional approaches fail to fully incorporate this aspect and network theory is seen as one possible explanation. Portfolios and matrices were then used to enable much of this theoretical part to be made practically useful.

Not all businesses in the 'forgotten cell' of the growth-share matrix will qualify for internationalization. But if 'psychic distances' have constrained activities to domestic arenas then searching for a place in an international network may be a less risky, more assured way of overcoming fear. Specific advantages may not be necessary as long as value added is brought to the chain. It may also be a quicker route than the traditional sequential chain.

Chapter 4

Low-share low-growth strategies in maturity and decline

INTRODUCTION

The argument, so far, is that divestment may not always be a justifiable choice for the 'dog' business (Thompson 1990). Divestment is only one of four possible 'disinvestment' options; the others being retrenchment, turnaround and liquidation. The recovery (Chapter 2) and internationalization (Chapter 3) strategies have been proposed for both the retrenchment and turnaround situations. If we could make a case for divestment being the most credible option for 'dogs' it would be here – where industry is in the mature/decline stage of its life cycle and businesses have only a finite period remaining before they head for liquidation. What then are the alternatives to divestment in this phase?

This chapter utilizes the life-cycle concept in a search for suggested strategic options during maturity and decline. These options are then critically examined for their role as alternatives to divestment.

LIFE-CYCLE APPROACHES TO STRATEGY FORMULATION

Like the BCG's growth-share matrix, the life-cycle concept has been held in high esteem by strategists seeking to analyse the dynamic evolution of products and industries (Levitt 1965; Buzzell 1966; Cox 1967; Wright 1971; Doyle 1976; Rink and Swan 1979; Harrigan 1980; Day 1981; Galbraith and Schendel 1982; Thietart and Vivas 1984; Anderson and Zeithaml 1984; Smith *et al.* 1985; Mascarenhas and Aaker 1989). Products and industry sales volumes are assumed to follow a four-stage biological cycle: introduction, growth, maturity and decline (Figure 4.1). Cash flow and profits vary, in

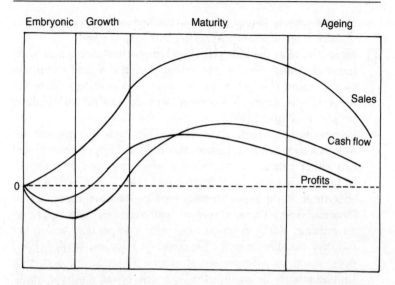

Embryonic   Growth   Maturity   Ageing

0

Sales

Cash flow

Profits

Figure 4.1 Sales, cash flows and profits over the industry life cycle
Source: Arthur D. Little, Inc.

their cycles, across the revenue profile. These latter cycles are important. Profit becomes positive only during the growth phase, peaking in maturity, and begins to recede in the decline phase, perhaps even turning negative. Cash flows, however, are significantly positive throughout both the mature and decline phases. These theoretical profiles provide the basis for different strategy options for the firm at each stage of the life cycle.

There are two chief concerns. First, that the performance variables (sales, profit, cash flow) follow such a natural evolution is, itself, controversial. Porter (1980) highlights a number of problems with what he describes as the 'grandfather of concepts' (life cycle).

1   Stage duration varies widely from industry to industry and it is difficult to tell what stage an industry is in at any one point in time. This dilutes the life cycle's value as a planning tool.
2   The S-shape pattern is not always representative of industry growth. Some industries skip stages, passing straight from growth to decline. Some industries manage to be rejuvenated after periods of decline (e.g. motorcycles and bicycles in the 1980s) through changing consumer tastes or demographics.

Macroeconomic depressions, can further mask the actual development stage of an industry (Hax and Majluf 1984).

3   Firms can alter the life-cycle shape themselves through product innovation and creative marketing (e.g. BMX and mountain bicycles) and through re-positioning: 'If a company takes the life cycle as given, it becomes an undesirable self-fulfilling prophesy' (Porter 1980).

4   Competition at each stage of the life cycle is different for different industries. Industries starting out highly concentrated can either remain so or, after a while, become fragmented. Industries starting out fragmented can either remain so (electronic component distribution) or become concentrated (automobiles). These divergent patterns can also apply to advertising, R&D expenditures, price competition and other industry variables over the life cycle. As Hax and Majluf (1984) note, when such important structural changes are occurring simultaneously in an industry, can any broad strategic implications possibly be drawn from the position of a business in the life cycle?

As Porter (1980) argues:

> And, except for industry growth rate, there is little or no underlying rationale for why the competitive changes associated with the life cycle will happen. Since actual industry evolution takes so many different paths, the life cycle pattern does not always hold, even if it is a common, or even the most common, pattern of evolution. Nothing in the concept allows us to predict when it will hold and when it will not.

Interestingly, this critique of the life cycle marked Porter's point of departure from the then conventional wisdom of analysing industries to his 'path-breaking packaging' of this analysis into a 5-force diagram covering entry barriers, supplier and buyer power, substitutes and competitive rivalry.

These criticisms do, however, raise the second concern, namely, the appropriateness of the strategy prescriptions at each phase of the life cycle. Even by the mid 1980s, despite numerous empirical studies, authors still claimed that this basic premise of the life cycle held (see, for instance, Thietart and Vivas 1984). Hofer (1975) who developed one of the most extensive theoretical profiles of the life cycle as it affects business strategy, stated strongly that:

The most fundamental variable in determining an appropriate business strategy is the stage of the PLC.

Major changes in business strategy are usually required during the three stages of the life cycle – introduction, maturity and decline.

The central part of his argument is that there are a set of descriptive prescriptions for each stage of the life cycle that relate strategies to performance. E.g.:

- *Introduction stage*: strategies emphasize a buyer focus, build on advertising and increased purchase frequency, high prices, product design, short production runs with high costs. This stage is characterized by few competitors, is high risk with low margins.
- *Growth stage*: buyer group widens, products differentiated by technical and performance characteristics, quality improvements, efficiencies in production and marketing with high advertising expenditure to create brand awareness, with mass distribution channels. This stage is characterized by many competitors, mergers, casualties, higher profits and falling prices.
- *Maturity stage*: focus on process efficiency, reduction in marketing and distribution costs, more product differentiation and market segmentation. Quality high, product standardized. Creative marketing to extend life cycle, packaging important. Mass production, long production runs, some over capacity. This stage is characterized by price competition, shake-outs, cyclicality, lower prices and margins.
- *Decline stage*: sophisticated buyers, little product differentiation, variable product quality. Cost control by cutting advertising and marketing efforts, specializing channels, simplifying production lines, relying on mass production, reducing differentiation and cutting R&D expenses. This stage is characterized by substantial over capacity therefore more exits and fewer competitors, falling prices and lower margins.

All these are essentially defensive actions. However, some authors have suggested more aggressive strategies based upon increasing investment and marketing during the latter stage (Hall 1980; Porter 1980; Harrigan 1980). These will be discussed below.

The above descriptions provide a broad general picture of life in each stage of the cycle. However there are a number of problems with their interpretation, particularly given the heterogeneity of the empirical research base that generated them. First, there are many contradictions in the research results due largely to differences in samples and sampling methods, and the choice of instrumental variables. Moreover, many of these studies take their data from the PIMS database (see Anderson and Payne 1978; Hambrick *et al.* 1982). One important limitation of this database is that it is restricted, in the main, to divisions of large organizations. Like the single business, these units have access to greater parental support and may be constrained by parental objectives and controls. Many facets of enterprise, ownership (see the early recoverers in Chapter 2), flexibility and speed of response that form the basis of, perhaps, more creative strategies may be absent.

Second, much of the research is partial – concentrating on one or more of the stages and rarely upon the whole of the life cycle. Even the most comprehensive (Anderson and Zeithaml 1984; Thietart and Vivas 1984) ignore the introductory stage. The most heavily researched stage is maturity and, consequently, successful strategies for high performance are difficult to unravel from the complexity of samples, methods and variables utilized.

Third, there is considerable controversy surrounding the nature of the performance objectives. The set of strategic variables at each stage of the life cycle may vary in their impact depending upon the specific objective chosen. For instance, inventories will be reduced to obtain a high rate of return on investment (ROI) objective and increased to promote a market-share gain objective. This could imply a trade-off between short-run (ROI) and long-run (market-share) objectives. However, some researchers (Rumelt and Wensley 1981; Hambrick *et al.* 1982) argue that these objectives are often compatible. In some growth markets, the combined effect of rapid revenue generation, higher value added, together with lower investment and expenses yields higher profits. Research has also shown that it is the higher profits that provide a fuel for higher growth rates (Grinyer and McKiernan 1992).

On the other hand, Thietart and Vivas (1984) in a comprehensive study relating strategies, environment and business characteristics, together with short-term (cash-flow) vs long-term (market-share) goals across the life cycle, show that strategies depend on goal orientation. Longer-term goals (market share) were associated with investment and asset increases. In contrast, cash-flow improves as both investments and assets are cut in the short term. There is, however, a pervasive effect on income and cash flow in the longer term from these kinds of cuts. Cash flow objectives therefore require different strategic actions at each stage than ROI objectives. Hence, it is essential to sort out the goals of the organization before any strategic actions can be deduced from the prescriptions of the life-cycle stages.

Fourth, given the controversy over the impact of conflicting objectives, there are some strategies that have proven to be successful across each stage of the life cycle, throwing into question Hofer's original, powerful assertion (above). Moreover, these strategies seem to be independent of environmental conditions and business characteristics (strategic posture and type of business). When market share is the goal, differentiation (of quality, product, value, price) leads industrial businesses to success regardless of their stage in the life cycle.

Fifth, strategic actions do not vary only with goal orientation, but also with the type of business. Industrial product firms may differentiate on product quality and service to satisfy sophisticated buyers while consumer product organizations rely more on market-orientated actions (sales forces) to improve their positions. Finally, as Thietart and Vivas (1984) have shown, there is no unique strategy associated with each stage. Effective strategies are a function of competitive posture, nature of the environment, corporate objectives, type of business as well as life-cycle stage.

Consequently, and contrary to Hofer's assertion, it is dangerous for the uninitiated to select automatic prescriptive strategy options from each stage of the life cycle. Other dimensions require construction and other tools and techniques are needed before a robust strategy formulation is complete.

The approach by Arthur D. Little (ADL), which helps overcome some of the difficulties mentioned above, is a wise starting point for this building process, stage by stage, whereby a profile of appropriate strategies for individual businesses across the life cycle can be established.

The logistical S-shape of the life cycle is translated into a familiar matrix form (compare the growth-share matrix and GE screen in Chapter 1). The competitive position defined in Table 4.1, is established to form the vertical axis. This is then positioned against the life cycle, denoting time on the horizontal axis. Figure 4.2 illustrates the primary phase of the analysis. Once a business unit is placed

Table 4.1 Criteria for classification of competitive position

---

1 'Dominant'
Dominant competitors are very rare. Dominance often results from a
quasi monopoly or from a strongly protected technological leadership.
2 'Strong'
Not all industries have dominant or strong competitors. Strong
competitors can usually follow strategies of their choice, irrespective of
their competitors' moves.
3 'Favourable'
When industries are fragmented, with no competitor clearly standing out,
the leaders tend to be in a favourable position.
4 'Tenable'
A tenable position can usually be maintained profitable through
specialization in a narrow or protected market niche. This can be a
geographic specialization or a product specialization.
5 'Weak'
Weak competitors can be intrinsically too small to survive independently
and profitable in the long term, given the competitive economics of their
industry, or they can be larger and potentially stronger competitors, but
suffering from costly past mistakes or from a critical weakness.

Source: Arthur D. Little, Inc. (1980)

within it (however subjective the decision), a 'natural' prescriptive
strategic objective is established, e.g. on market share, investment
requirements or cash-flow expectations. In turn, these objectives
suggest specific strategic options shown in Figure 4.3 for market
share. These two figures are only the start of a lengthy, organized
and well-structured methodology developed by ADL and based
firmly on the life-cycle concept.[1] The danger is that this type of
rigidity can constrain creative thinking, boxing-in the available
strategic options. The emergence of innovation could be stifled in
the hands of naive users (compare growth-share matrix in Chapter
1). ADL do overcome many of these weaknesses by operating a host
of techniques alongside this family of portfolios to fortify their
analysis (a commentary well versed in Chapter 1 and repeated by
Wind (1982) and Anderson and Zeithaml (1984)).

Despite many of the limitations discussed, provided care is taken
in building up a stage by stage analysis, using a variety of tools (e.g.
ADL), the result should be a highly creative and consistent one,
representing good practice in both strategic planning and strategic
management. With these cautions registered, it is now appropriate

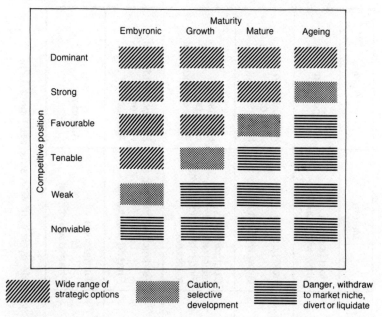

Figure 4.2 The life-cycle portfolio matrix
Source: Arthur D. Little, Inc.

to analyse the more aggressive strategies available to the maturing/declining organizations presented by this literature.

CHARACTERISTICS OF INDUSTRY MATURITY

The previous section warns against the injudicious adherence to a life-cycle analogy and to any prescriptive strategies based upon its stages. So what do we do with the 'dogs' in low-growth, low-share businesses? Growth peaks where markets and industries mature, although there will be pockets of both positive and negative growth in these mature market segments. Hence, the mature phase ought to contain the most businesses in the bottom half of a conventional growth-share matrix – as cash cows or dogs. Our concern, specifically, at this stage is with the low-share businesses when growth is low or has tailed off. First, we examine the characteristics of maturity:

The law of the jungle changes as maturity comes and hostility

	Embryonic	Growth	Mature	Ageing
Dominant	All out push for share Hold position	Hold position Hold share	Hold position Grow with industry	Hold position
Strong	Attempt to improve position All out push for share	Attempt to improve position Push for share	Hold position Grow with industry	Hold position or Harvest
Favourable	Selective or all out push for share Selective attempt to improve position	Attempt to improve position Selective push for share	Custodial or maintenance Find niche and attempt to protect	Harvest or Phased withdrawal
Tenable	Selectively push for position	Find niche and protect it	Find niche and hang on or Phased withdrawal	Phased withdrawal or Abandon
Weak	Up or Out	Turnaround or Abandon	Turnaround or Phased withdrawal	Abandon

Figure 4.3 Strategic position in terms of market share suggested by the life-cycle portfolio matrix (see Figure 4.2).

Source: Arthur D. Little, Inc.

intensifies. In such a jungle the range of strategic options narrows, requiring both an early warning of the coming hostility and an early strategic repositioning for a company to survive and prosper.   (Hall 1982)

Contrary to a widely held view, the mature stage is not a reflection of demand and product stability, characterized by low levels of competition and slow change (Hofer 1975; Scherer 1980). For most organizations, maturity is the most important phase. Introduction and growth may be short lived, but maturity can continue indefinitely. It is a complex phase, where fundamental market conditions alter radically. Schofield and Arnold (1988) assert that the long mature stage is in fact made up of four further distinctive phases – late growth, early maturity, mid maturity and late maturity. Each one has its own specific dynamics – especially price which fluctuates markedly between these sub-phases.

Moreover, Baden-Fuller *et al.* (1988) have argued that competition can be intense behind this 'mask of maturity'. The structure of demand can show significant change over time and, although the product may be well established, the source of cost advantage may change from scale-driven to non-scale-driven factors (e.g. European machine industry, textiles and knitwear, cutlery etc.). Hence many existing theories of competition in traditional industries require modification, as a single, static model is not adequate to describe the whole of the mature phase of the industry's life cycle.

SUCCESSFUL STRATEGIES IN HOSTILE MATURITY

Hall (1982) examined 64 firms in 8 American mature industries in the 1970s and 1980s at a time when slow growth, high inflation, increased regulation and import penetration were creating an environment of turbulence and hostility. These industries – steel, tyres and rubber, heavy-duty trucks, construction and materials handling equipment, automotives, domestic appliances, beer and cigarettes – witnessed their share of failures and exits as the environmental impact took its toll. In heavy truck manufacture alone, Chrysler bowed out, Diamond Reo was in bankruptcy, White closed to receivership, while Mack and International Harvester lost significant market share and both searched actively for foreign assistance. A similar picture emerged in the other industries. Balanced against these disasters, however, were firms that performed well in hostile circumstances. In fact, the leading performers in each industry outperformed the Fortune 1,000 index on factors such as the return on equity, return on capital and revenue growth over the same period. Their strategies shared common characteristics across industries, were continuous and long-term. Organizations, single-mindedly, tried to achieve one or both of the following objectives:

1   *Lowest delivered cost position* relative to competition, coupled with both an acceptable delivered quality and a pricing policy to gain profitable volume and market share growth (e.g. Ford, General Motors, Whirlpool, Miller).

2   *Highest product/service quality differentiated position* relative to competition, coupled with both an acceptable delivered cost structure and a pricing policy to gain margin sufficient to fund reinvestment in product/service differentiation (e.g. National Steel, Michelin, John Deere, Daimler-Benz).

Caterpillar (construction equipment) and Philip Morris (cigarettes) managed to successfully achieve both. All these successful companies had a clear, consistent purpose fostered by careful strategic analysis and:

> avoided simplistic adherence to doctrinaire approaches towards strategy formulation which comes from the naive application of such management tools as share-growth matrices (suggesting that mature market segments should be milked or harvested) or experience curve/PIMS planning models (suggesting that high market share and/or lowest cost, vertically integrated production is the key to success in mature industries). Instead ... the performance leaders made investment decisions which frequently conflicted with these doctrinaire theories.
>
> (Hall 1982)

Hall's results make powerful reading:

1   Doctrinaire prescriptions, e.g. 'milking' in maturity, were not being followed by performance leaders. On the contrary, they aggressively reinvested in core businesses rather than directed assets to diversification (as might be prescribed).

2   Low-cost production is not essential in order to prosper in mature markets (contrary to experience-curve predictions). High sustainable returns can come from investment in an average cost, highly differentiated position.

3   Vertical integration is not necessary to exploit cost leadership in mature markets. Performance leaders concentrated on efficiencies in process technology at one stage in the value chain, e.g. Ford.
4   High market share and accumulated experience are not essential for cost leadership.

The latter point is crucial for the theme of this book. In fact, 50 per cent of Hall's low-cost producers, e.g. Inland Steel, Whirlpool, Miller and Philip Morris, achieved their successful positions without high relative market share. They had focused on modern automated process technology in their plants and invested heavily in distribution systems to gain scale economies and other cost reductions in their delivery systems.

These strategies of low cost and differentiation for 'followers' rather than leading market share organizations in a mature market have been stressed by Porter (1985) and, more recently, by Thompson and Strickland (1990). The growth-share doctrinaire prescriptions and the abundant analyses of PIMS data have both been instrumental in promoting the myth surrounding the drive for large market share. The often used, and yet famous, quotation from Buzzell *et al* (1975) that: 'on the average, a difference of 10% points in market share is accompanied by a difference of about 5% points in pre-tax ROI' shares a large responsibility for inculcating the belief within managers and consultants that low market share businesses must either increase their market shares or withdraw from the industry. There is no dispute that a large market share can endow an organization with several distinct advantages, e.g. in branding, scale economies and bargaining power in the value-added chain. However, some circumstances, e.g. frequent product change, rapid technology advances, regulatory intervention, can mitigate against the favourable impact of large market shares on profitability. In addition, it should be remembered that the PIMS relationship between market share and profitability was a correlation between the variables and not a causation.

SUCCESSFUL LOW-SHARE STRATEGIES

Fortunately, in parallel with the explosion of PIMS-based research came a softer eruption of the literature on small and medium-sized enterprises. This research provided considerable detail of low share/

high-performance organizations whose strengths lay in specialization, local focus, high-quality product and customer service, narrower product lines and flexibility of response to consumer demand. Hamermesh *et al.* (1978) were amongst the first authors to highlight the consistent out-performance of large rivals by the low-share 'followers' that Hall (1982) confirmed. They attacked the growth-share prescriptions, especially those of divestment claiming that:

> Although each classification system has its nuances, all such systems share the same shortcoming: they define strategy at such a high level of abstraction that it becomes meaningless. A successful business strategy must be specific, precise and far ranging. It should state the markets in which the business will compete, the products that will be sold, their performance and price characteristics, the way in which they will be produced and distributed and the method of financing. By taking the attention of corporate executives away from these essential details and instead focusing on abstraction, many planning systems do a great disservice.   (Hamermesh *et al.* 1978)

Unfortunately, their work is limited to three case studies (Burroughs, Crown Cork and Seal and Union Camp) and so their generalized strategies for success in low-share businesses – of segmentation, efficient use of R&D, a concentration on innovation and driving leadership – lack sufficient support.

The necessary underpinning was provided by Woo and Cooper[2] (1982) who examined strategies in 40 effective low-share businesses (≥ 20% ROI and ≤ 20% market share relative to 3 largest competitors combined), 39 effective high-share (≤ 20% ROI and ≤ 125% relative market share) and 47 ineffective low share businesses (≤ 5% ROI and ≤ 20% relative market share).

Using multivariate analysis on a PIMS database, they established the following results:

1   Effective low-share business (ELBs) were in product market environments characterized by slow, real growth and infrequent product changes, involving the sale of standardized industrial components and supplies, without the provision of a high level of custom features or auxiliary services. There was a high purchase frequency, high value added and large numbers of competitors.

This result alone challenged the doctrinaire prescriptions which suggested that low-share businesses should locate in growth markets and provide specialist services and custom features.

2   Ineffective low-share businesses (ILBs) tended to operate in the same product-market environments. So why did they not perform as well?

There was a clear difference in the way that each did business at the competitive level. ELBs concentrated on high product quality at a lower price, careful cost control with limited spending on marketing, R&D and vertical integration. On the other hand ILBs tried to do much the same as the effective high-share businesses, taking an aggressive stance of broad product lines, intense marketing, R&D and vertical integration. As the authors point out: 'Their scale of activities was not large enough to support all these activities; their resources had been spread too thinly' (Woo and Cooper 1981).

Although their research has limitations – those associated with the PIMs database (see earlier), solely cross-sectional, focusing on industrial rather than consumer products and with restricted sampling (inclusion of ineffective high-share would balance the sampling frame and facilitate a more even comparison of the results) – it established clearly that low-share, higher performance was alive and well. Hall (1982) confirmed the durability of these results during periods of hostility.

As the research on low-share businesses has become established in the literature it has enabled writers such as Kotler (1984), Porter (1985) and Thompson and Strickland (1990) to develop a set of available strategic choices. These are particularly appropriate where larger competitors do not have distinct advantages associated with high market shares, e.g. cost advantages. In these circumstances, smaller, 'follower' firms have more strategic flexibility and should be able to pursue any of the following options successfully:

1   *Vacant niche strategy*: based on the primary principle of not attacking leaders head-on and going where they are absent, into neglected niches, e.g. regional airlines serving less popular towns and 'own brand' manufacturers who can survive alongside the giants.

2   *Specialist strategy*: a focus on carefully selected product markets, no broad-line range, adding value that appeals to certain customers, e.g. Canada Dry in ginger ale, tonic and soda water.

3 *Quality strategy*: the key here is product quality, marketing efforts are focused on quality consciousness and performance-orientated buyers through craftsmanship, frequent product innovation and close customer contact, e.g. Tiffany in diamonds and jewellery, Bally in shoes.

4 *Content follower strategy*: avoid attempts to steal customers from the leader or undercut the leader on price, opting for a focus or differentiation to avoid any of the leaders' direct paths, e.g. Burroughs in its avoidance of IBM by focusing on applications for specific customer groups, tailoring R&D, with an emphasis on profits rather than market share and cautious, efficient management.

5 *Growth via acquisition*: gain share by merging or acquiring rivals, e.g. accounting and consultancy firms in the 1980s such as Coopers & Lybrand, Deloitte.

6 *Distinctive image strategy*: creating a reputation to stand out from competitors, e.g. lowest price (Kwiksave in the UK, food retailing), prestige quality at a good price (Jaguar cars), superior customer service (British Midland airline), unique product attributes (Apple's user-friendly computers), creative advertising (Guinness).

These competitive strategies at the business level are essentially based on focus and differentiation. Together with Hall's 1982 results on low-cost success strategies, low-share businesses can draw creatively on all three of Porter's (1980) original generic strategies rather than be constrained by matrix prescriptions. Clearly, there is much that the low share business can do to box out of its dog cell.

END-GAME STRATEGIES

In Chapters 2 and 3, the focus was on rejuvenation or revitalization of businesses. So far in this chapter we have focused on the life-cycle stage of maturity and, in particular, successful strategies for low-share businesses. However, when businesses reach the decline stage of the life cycle there is a certain inevitability of death. Portfolio prescriptions amount to no more than 'milking' or 'withdrawal'. In these low positive or negative overall demand growth situations, how can the 'dogs' survive?

Such environments of inevitable decline have become known as 'end-game' situations.[3] The end game marks the final stages of a business's life. It begins after the growth of industry-wide sales has levelled out. This decline phase can continue for decades. For instance, the last TV set containing vacuum tubes was manufactured (USA) in 1974. The legacy was a replacement tube market feeding over twenty years of production for television sets: a sizeable market of price-insensitive demand which enabled the six leading tube manufacturers, through efficient management, to continue in operation for a further two decades, reaping stable and high returns. Harrigan (1980) found that over 33 per cent of a sample of declining businesses returned an average of over 35 per cent return on capital employed. A similar picture is painted in the UK television rental section described by Rafferty (1987).

Although the end game can be of long duration, profits may not be so large and competition may not be so stable for all businesses. Competition can become intense, through, for instance, price wars, as businesses fight for an increased share of a decreasing market. Hence, it is important to understand the factors influencing the dynamics of competition before any successful strategies can be created for the end-game player.

The following analytical steps (adopted and developed from Porter 1980) can help determine the strategies for businesses in end games.

1   Can decline be predicted?
2   Will demand conditions facilitate a favourable decline phase?
3   Can the exit barriers for all businesses be analysed, influenced and exit predicted?
4   What are the relative strengths and weaknesses of all the remaining competitors in addressing the residual pockets of demand?

Predicting decline

The most respected authorities on declining industries (Porter 1980; Harrigan 1980; 1988; Hamermesh and Silk 1979; Robinson 1986) all stress that a successful competitive posture in decline depends upon the amount of preparation an organization undertakes in the phase of late maturity. Prediction of decline is crucial. Over 60 per cent of industries within mature economies (Western Europe, Japan, USA) are expressing slow, zero or negative demand growth for their products. Some of these are illustrated in Table 4.2.

Harrigan (1990) has argued that many managers responsible for businesses in these mature industries fail to noice that demand is stagnant. Their focus is upon revenues rather than unit volume. Individual business output is rarely compared with industrial output and, consequently, these managements fail to see the coming of the end game.

This form of myopia can be particularly acute if economies are experiencing an upward trend in their business cycle. Surrounded by other managers in different industries that portray all the symptoms of managerial 'hubris' associated with growth phases (e.g. business confidence, expansionism through acquisition), managers

Table 4.2. Industries suffering a levelling-off or decline in volume

Adding machines	Lead pencils and crayons
Baby foods and baby products	Leather belting for machines
Barbed wire fencing	Leather-tanning services
Basic petrochemicals	Mainframe computers
Beer	Manual typewriters
Buttons and hooks	Millinery and millinery blocks
Canned peas, other vegetables	Paper mills
Cigars, cigarettes, pipe tobacco	Passenger-liner services
Commercial-passenger aeroplane propellers	Percolator coffeemakers
Cork products	Permanent-wave machines
Corsets, girdles, and brassieres	Petroleum refining
Creamery butter, cheese, whole milk	Gramophone records and players
Nappies and rubber panties	Pocket watches
Electronic receiving tubes	Sewing machines
Evaporated milk	Slide rules
Farming machinery	Steam locomotives and passenger train cars
Fountain pens	Steam radiators
Gas-lighting fixtures	Straight razors
Hand-held irons and ironing boards	Sugar
Hardwood flooring	Trolley-car services
Harpoons	Venetian blinds
Hot breakfast cereals	Vinyl gramophone records
Lace and net goods	Washboards
	Whisky distilling
	Wringer washing machines

Source: Harrigan (1990)

of potential end-game businesses are less likely to take immediate action on their current position. (The opposite also occurs – economic depressions can be erroneously interpreted as the setting in of a decline phase).

Correct prediction of the decline phase is therefore crucial. It enables the organization to reposition strategically to replenish, reinvest or rationalize its asset base and ensure that suitable general managers are appointed if the intention is to remain.

According to Harrigan and Porter (1983) the following steps should be covered in maturity when a business is preparing for the end game:

- Minimize investments or other actions that will increase exit barriers unless these are essential.
- Increase flexibility of assets so they can accept different raw materials or produce related products.
- Spot segments that will endure throughout the decline phase and occupy them early.
- Create customer switching costs in these segments.

The analysis of demand (below) is crucial in assessing the likely competitive dynamics of the decline phase, deciding on whether to compete and, if so, how to re-position strategically to do so.

Predicting demand conditions[4]

Causes of decline need to be isolated before predictions on its rate and volatility, and the subsequent degree of competition, can be assessed. The general causes of decline can be split into technological (change, product obsolescence, substitutes, new raw materials), socio-demographic (demographic trends – baby booms, conservation policies), and fashion (life style changes, styling). In general, technological declines are far more predictable, especially where businesses understand the substitute technologies. Declines precipitated by socio-demographic and fashion changes introduce a great uncertainty into the prediction process.

Other variables

Besides the volatility of decline, other variables can be measured that highlight the likelihood of a favourable or unfavourable climate.

These are, for example:

Managerial perception

Managers seeing the possibility of rejuvenation may hold on tighter to their position, creating uncertainty and a higher degree of competition. On the other hand, a general acceptance throughout the industry of decline can lead to a more orderly process.

Structure of remaining demand

If the remaining demand is price-insensitive (e.g. premium products), it allows organizations to increase price to maintain profits in the face of decreasing sales. If a product has a direct substitute it becomes price-sensitive and costs can no longer be fully covered by price rises. Any subsequent price war can be extremely destructive.

The above features provide only a partial determinant of the factors impinging upon favourable or unfavourable decline phases. This analysis needs reinforcement by careful study of the barriers which may prevent businesses from withdrawing easily from their current market position.

Predicting and influencing exit barriers

A timely exit from the industry can be thwarted by the existence of barriers which can become insurmountable for some businesses and strongly influence the extent of competition in the decline stage. Exit barriers manifest themselves in a variety of forms (see Table 4.3). Most critical are those barriers relating to specialized assets with little or no alternative use that restrict a business's strategic flexibility. They can probably only be sold to competitors who wish to stay in the industry.

The manager's objective is to win the game of 'exit barrier manipulation'. The first move is to ease the way forward for their organization by lowering their indigenous exit barriers if analysis predicts extreme volatility and uncertainty in the end game and, consequently, they do not wish to participate (see Table 4.4). The second move is to influence the barriers to exit of their competitors (both to expedite their exit and to acquire their assets and customer lists and thereby increase market share), if analysis suggests that the end-game environment is going to be favourable for their businesses and they have decided to compete (see Table 4.5): 'The last iceman

Table 4.3 Exit barriers

Specialised assets (little or no alternative use)

Accounting loss treatments
- Poor performance undermines confidence in management's capabilities
- Valuation induces firms to prolong presence in industry

Strategic exit barriers
- Quality image, shared customers, shared physical facilities or other shared strategic facilities
- Centrepiece of related strategies impinging on corporate image
- Customers may be cut off, could harm firm in other businesses

Managerial exit barriers
- Emotional (prestige) investment on brands
- Turf battles (interdepartmental transfers)

Costs of exit
- Labour settlements
- Dismantling costs

Social barrier
- Effect on local economy
- Effect on unemployment rate
- Conservation issues

Table 4.4 Lowering indigenous exit barriers

- *Accounting*
Create reserves to offset the cost of write-off losses on disposal where allowed

- *Technological*
Trade-off highly specialized plant and equipment for more flexible assets that can take other raw materials and produce related products

- *Financial*
Lease. Do not purchase

- *Multinational*
Plan to move assets abroad on a scheduled basis, forcing 'jump-off' points of re-evaluation to fund new assets

- *Planning*
Routinely evaluate whether to exit from a business when it falls below a prescribed level. Unlock declining businesses from others

Source: Developed from Harrigan (1982)

in mature industries strives to decrease competitors' exit barriers by acquiring their assets and serving their customers' (Harrigan 1990).

Predicting capabilities

Rafferty (1987), using the investment depreciation ratio[5] and the rate of cash flow,[6] provides a detailed matrix-based analysis for studying competitors' financial exit barriers and hence their vulnerability to specific decline stage strategies. The former ratio, by measuring the level of investment in fixed assets, predicts the conservatism associated with a businesses-depreciation policy. The latter ratio gives an estimate as to the investment profile of a particular business by measuring the cash flows generated from its asset base. The result of combining these two ratios is a two by two matrix which positions all businesses in the declining industry relative to each other (see Figure 4.4). This display enables 'what if' type questions to be asked about each firm's vulnerability to a specific decline stage strategy, e.g.:

> B's strategic position is a strong one as investment levels are low while cash generation is high. Barriers to entry, in terms of the need to sustain specific returns on investment, are less demanding than those faced by company A. However, A's position is most vulnerable with low cash and high investments, exit barriers are formidable and probably insurmountable if faced with a rapid rate of market decline. Hence B would steal market share from A by leading a downward price spiral where A's ability to compete is handicapped by its need to maintain adequate ROIs. An

Table 4.5 Lowering competitors' exit barriers

- Acquire their physical plant or assets
- Offer to service and supply replacement parts to their customers
- If a supplier appears eager to help a competitor, offer to purchase more from that supplier
- Alert regulatory agencies of competitors' transgressions, particularly in pollution control
- Start a price war providing strengths exit, e.g. if you face price insensitivity
- Go public in plea for their exit

Source: Developed from Harrigan (1982)

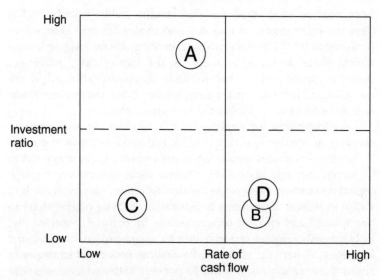

Figure 4.4 Movement of cash flow against investment ratio
Source: Rafferty (1987)

inability to do so could have ramifications for its share price and cost of capital. C will do best to harvest its position and may become the prime acquisition candidate as excess capacity dominates the declining market.

This type of analysis, coupled with a broader SWOT approach, yields significant information for 'simulation' analysis of strategy choices and their effect on rivals. It also enables individual managers to analyse and identify the optimum strategy in their particular circumstances.

STRATEGIC OPTIONS IN THE END GAME

Strategy selection means matching internal strengths and weaknesses to the end-game environment. The strengths and weaknesses in the previous stages of growth and maturity may no longer be appropriate for sustaining a competitive advantage in the decline phase. Success depends upon the ability to serve the residual pockets of demand that remain and the ability to handle the varying degrees of competition that may follow. The matrix (Figure 4.5) provides an approximate guide to strategy choice. This depends upon whether the prior analysis established a highly certain, stable, orderly decline (favourable) or degree of volatility and rivalry between competitors (unfavourable). Table 4.6 provides a useful guide for judging favourability of the declining industry. In the former case, indigenous strengths should lead to a drive for leadership position through investment; in the latter case, this strategy is likely to fail and rationalization and niche focus are probably the best prescription.

This framework for analysis should facilitate an *early* strategic decision on whether to compete in the end game and how to do this. If this decision entails remaining in the industry the strategy has to be forced through aggressively. Strong clear signals, say through capital investment, early on in the decline phase, may be enough to nudge indecisive competitors to exit early, enabling market share to be captured and effective competition to be reduced. Significantly, in Harrigan's original research into 61 organizations in end-game situations, 92 per cent of them following the prescribed strategies in Figure 4.5 were successful, while 85 per cent of those businesses who did not follow them failed. Such is the difference in predictability when

Competitive strength for remaining demand pockets

	High	Medium	Low
Favourable	Increase or Hold	Hold or Shrink	Shrink or Milk
Industry decline structure			
Unfavourable	Shrink or Milk	Milk or Divest Now	Divest Now

Figure 4.5 Strategic options in end game

Sources: Adapted from Harrigan (1980) and Harrigan and Porter (1983)
Notes: Favourable and unfavourable conditions described in Table 4.6 and accompanying strategies in Table 4.7.

Table 4.6 Attractiveness potential of declining industry

Speed of decline	Very slow	Rapid or erratic
Certainty of decline	Very predictable patterns	Great uncertainty, erratic patterns
Pockets of enduring demand	Several or major ones	No niches
Product differentiation	Brand loyalty	Commodity-like products
Price stability	Stable, price premiums attainable	Very unstable, pricing below costs
Exit barriers Reinvestment requirements	None	High, often mandatory and involving capital assets
Excess capacity	Little	Substantial
Asset age	Mostly old assets	Sizable new assets and old ones not retired
Resale markets for assets	Easy to convert or sell	No markets available, substantial costs to retire
Shared facilities	Few free-standing plants	Substantial and inter-connected with important businesses
Vertical integration	Little	Substantial
'Single product' competitors	None	Several large competitors
Rivalry determinants Customer industries	Fragmented, weak	Strong bargaining power
Customer switching costs	High	Minimal
Diseconomies of scale	None	Substantial
Dissimilar strategic groups	Few	Several in same target markets

Source: Adapted from Harrigan and Porter (1983)

Table 4.7 Generic strategies pursued by firms in end game

Strategy	Mandate
Increase the investment	Dominate viable niche of remaining customers
Hold investment level	Re-invest to maintain posture until uncertainty is resolved
Shrink selectively	Prune lines of products and groups of customers served to position self in most lucrative niches
Milk the investment	Harvest cash flow without regard for market position
Divest now!	Sell or abandon assets as quickly as possible

Source: Adapted from Harrigan (1982)

prescriptions are based upon matrices underpinned by rigorous research rather than those underpinned by curious ideology.

REFINING END-GAME STRATEGIES

Harrigan's original research (1980) was undertaken for a doctoral thesis at the Harvard Business School supervised by Michael Porter. Since then, both academics have become widely influential. Much of their later research in the 1980s (see Harrigan 1988) has confirmed many of these earlier results on end-game strategies. Their results overturned much of the conventional matrix prescriptions on corporate decline. They suggest that the adoption of a more aggressive posture, after systematic analysis, can yield high rewards. Robinson (1986) has lent weight to these assertions. In his study, he analysed the strategies of over three hundred industrial businesses experiencing negative real growth, from data in the PIMS base.

Using cluster analysis, the declining businesses were separated into three groups, each with distinct characteristics, e.g. fragmentation vs concentration in market structure, market share and customer profile (see Table 4.8). In general, the results show:

Table 4.8 Different types of market environment (differences significant at the 5 per cent level)

	Group I	Group II	Group III
Industry and market			
Number of competitors	19	8	4
Big four market share	42%	76%	94%
Market position			
Market share rank	2.4	2.2	1.5
Market share	11%	23%	43%
Relative market share	48%	53%	122%
Customer profile			
Number of end users	2,500	1,400	400
Number of immediate customers	630	250	130
Purchase amount immediate customers	$4,000	$10,000	$10,000
Purchase interval	5 weeks	7 weeks	10 weeks

Source: Robinson (1986)

1   That average profit and cash flows were not significantly different in the three groups.
2   That given the results in (1) above, and the differences in market share illustrated in Table 4.8, the latter variable is not decisive in declining markets. Other factors like the number of competitors and customer power are equally influential. *Matrices based on market share do not provide appropriate prescriptions for the decline phase.*
3   That capital intensity, employee ratios, marketing effort, cost structure and R&D do not differ significantly between the three groups.
4   That, with respect to both profit (ROI) and cash flows, a number of factors are related to good performance in all these types of markets:
    •   a strong market position;
    •   low capital intensity;
    •   high relative product quality;
    •   low purchase or manufacturing costs.

Because the results for cash flows are similar to those for profitability it appears that businesses having a high cash flow generally achieve this through high profitability, rather than by running down their capital base, market share, sales force, or R&D expenditure. This result is consistent with those in the field of corporate recovery (see Chapter 2) where a cutting back on overhead expenses (e.g. marketing budgets) in a recession is a confirmed route to the graveyard. In addition, high relative product quality was also influential for goals of high market share confirming its role in the wider PIMS research studies.

5　That, in fragmented markets, low advertising expenditure is beneficial to both profitability and cash flows but, in concentrated markets, pricing becomes the key variable.

Robinson went a stage further than both Harrigan and Porter. He compared the average profitability and cash flow of businesses in these declining markets with over six hundred industrial firms in growing markets. Surprisingly, there was no difference in the average performance figures between the two markets.

The evidence on performance in declining markets is strong. Through systematic analysis and the identification of niches in late maturity that will have enduring qualities throughout the decline phase, aggressive rather than defensive strategies can lead to high rates of return. The key advice seems to be:

- Recognize decline and prepare.
- Avoid price wars and wars of attrition behind high exit barriers.
- Don't harvest without definite strengths; keep up quality and service.
- Decline is an *opportunity* not a *threat*.

MANAGEMENT FOR DECLINE

It was noted in Chapter 2 (recovery) that there are managerial styles appropriate to specific stages in the life of a business. For instance, during crises, autocratic styles tend to be better. Whereas in a consolidation phase, the more effective leader is likely to be a democratic one. The decline phase is exceptional. It is still heavily coloured by the myth of managing a dog. This view normally permeates down the division from the top, making it impossible to get managers excited or motivated enough to try anything new. Moreover, an organization's most talented and aggressive managers are usually assigned to their rapidly growing divisions leaving stagnating divisions to less aggressive and less competent managers. Less competent managers clearly complicate the demands already imposed by decline.

Hence the choice of management through the decline phase is going to be a crucial element in implementing the creative strategies necessary to reap the higher returns available. Functional specialists, for instance marketing people who concentrate solely on increasing sales, are probably inappropriate. Conservatism or lack of enterprise have also to be avoided. Hamermesh and Silk (1979) have suggested that the most effective managers for decline are experienced general managers whose futures are closely linked to the success of the divisions through incentive packages based firmly upon the size of ROIs achieved. To quote one senior industrialist in their survey:

> I try to assign these [stagnant] businesses to people who are ready for their second or third general manager job. These are real good positions to test the flexibility of these people. Also, I think by assigning talented people we get a leg up on our competitors who may be downplaying these businesses.
>
> (quoted in Hamermesh and Silk 1979)

SUMMARY

This chapter has examined the situations of low market share and low (or negative) growth businesses, i.e. the dogs. Research has shown repeatedly that high market share is not necessary to achieve high ROIs and high cash flows. Low-cost production, focus or differentiation were shown to be successful generic strategies available to low share businesses. Further, when growth has levelled off or begins to decline, conventional prescriptive strategies like 'harvest' or 'withdrawal' can be too automatic and defensive. End game is an opportunity for the enterprising business. Through careful analysis in advance of the decline, strategies yielding high returns, perhaps for decades, can be achieved. As discussed in Chapter 2 and Chapter 3 above, there is much that the dogs can do to help themselves.

In the survey of research covered in this chapter, one further point requires stressing. Time and again, conventional prescriptive strategies derived from naive, simplistic matrices have proved to be erroneous – a story, whose origins can be traced back to Chapter 1.

However, when matrices are the result of solid rigorous research programmes (see Harrigan 1980) the recommendations can be highly efficient. It is probably too cynical an approach to simply ignore every matrix in strategy or marketing. It is necessary to question their roots and, as was highlighted in Chapter 1, to use them judiciously, supported by fortifying frameworks.

Chapter 5

Concluding comments

INTRODUCTION

The mood of this book has been one of positive aggression. A mood to generate creative strategic thinking and avoid the strictures of conventional matrix-based prescriptions for action. The myopic following of these instructions could mean missing opportunities to devise much more exciting, challenging and rewarding strategies for businesses which have been condescendingly referred to as dogs.

Chapter 1 was instrumental in exploring the difficulties and dangers associated with the technique of the 1970s – the growth-share matrix. This still has a useful role to play if used with wisdom and, especially, if accompanied by other tools and techniques. Yet, even in the 1990s, research has shown that it is still taught on management courses in a non-critical manner. Although time and change may have eroded many of its early foundations, it should not be ejected from the strategic analysis tool-box. Uncritical users, however, should heed the warnings. Automatic prescriptions of divestment are not appropriate for all dogs.

Chapter 2 examined the manner in which businesses could recover at all stages of relative decline – not least the one closely associated with turnaround and death. For this chapter, and for the remainder of the book, the manner in which decisions are made in organizations are described in a general model. The model performed well when matched with empirical data. Research into strategic decision-making processes held the key to answering the critique against automatic prescriptions. Data from decision-process studies indicated that the uncritical application of growth-share matrices neither occurred unfailingly in practice, nor represented necessarily what successful firms did. In the largest empirical study of strategic decision making in Britain, Hickson *et al.* (1986) conclusively demonstrated the wide range of strategic options and choices available beyond the determinism of growth-share prescriptions. In the present series of books, Wilson (1992) shows how specific strategies (those concerned with organizational change) have been equally beset by uncritical thinking and warns against recipe-bound and overly deterministic perspectives. Recoveries are possible for most businesses. The secret is in anticipation through environmental awareness, avoidance of rigid thinking, of previously successful recipes or ways of doing business. A need to stay open of mind, fresh of thought and a willingness to challenge and take risks are essential ingredients for rejuvenation.

Chapter 3 contained, arguably, a more adventurous strategy suggestion for the dogs. Recovery (Chapter 2) and internationalization (Chapter 3) are both closely related in practice and not necessarily mutually exclusive strategies (see Tube Investments case later in this chapter). The traditional, sequential model of internationalization, from exports, through licensing to foreign direct investment is still a popular choice, reducing uncertainty by incremental progress. However, as global competition changes, as less-developed countries catch up more quickly with developed countries, sequential change becomes limited in its explanation of the growth in internationalization by acquisition. Moreover, network analysis, which copes well in its explanations of acquisitive strategies, also lends itself to an easier and quicker entry to international markets than sequential change. If domestic markets are saturated then foreign fields may be one alternative solution to survival for many low-share, low-growth businesses.

Chapter 4 examines strategies for these low-share and low-growth businesses where automatic prescriptions of divestment held possibly their greatest credence – i.e. at the late mature or decline phase of an industry's life cycle. Life-cycle analogies were themselves challenged for authenticity and for throwing up their own automatic prescriptions. Yet where industries could be identified as being in late maturity or decline, successful strategies were clearly identified. Notably, these were not based on high market shares. The identification of successful strategies requires good anticipation, analysis and, most important, a positive mental attitude. Late-mature and end-game situations are opportunities and not threats. Skilful, enterprising general managers can earn high rates of return by a creative exploitation of the end-game structural features, e.g. exit barriers.

The unit of analysis throughout the book has been on the 'dog' business in a wider portfolio of businesses. Inevitably, there has been some variation. It is difficult to consider recovery without analysis of the whole group of businesses that constitutes the portfolio. Nor is it possible to isolate the international expansion of a low-share/low-growth domestic business from any international activities or networks that the wider group of businesses is involved with. Moreover, in the discussion of specific strategies for low-share businesses and end game it is essential to move from corporate decisions on product/market characteristics (e.g. type of product, geographic location etc.) to competitive strategy decisions at the business level (e.g. relative price, quality, sales force, advertising) to discover the detail beneath the broader generic terms like 'milk', 'hold' or 'harvest'. To draw the story to a close, it is useful to tie the four chapters together in discussing the case of Tube Investments.

INTEGRATING CASE: TUBE INVESTMENTS

In the late 1970s, Tube Investments (TI), a long-standing British engineering group, had a diversified business portfolio spreading from 'bicycles to kettles'. Its most profitable and enduring division – domestic appliances – produced a wide assortment of fridges, washing machines, gas cookers, water heaters and kettles, many with well-known brand names, e.g. Creda, New World, Russell Hobbs. TI had other divisions involved in steel tube, toys and cycles (including the international brand Raleigh), aluminium and specialized engineering. Returns throughout the 1970s were declining in real terms and relative to the industry. The UK recession, beginning in 1978–9, took a heavy toll on organizational performance. TI was on the brink of disaster, desperate for cash in order to survive. A new chief executive officer (Ronald Utiger) arrived in 1982. Actions were taken to sell off the prestigious head office in Birmingham and relocate to smaller premises in London, to rationalize its activities (especially commodities – aluminium and some tube), shedding huge sections of its labour force, and to streamline the inefficient and archaic management and board structures that impeded efficient decision making.

TI began to recover sharply. Its domestic appliances division had held up well throughout the recession and had a strong supportive organizational culture, supported by profit-related incentive schemes for its management (see Wilson 1992). However, toys and bicycles continued to lose money with specialized engineering just showing signs of improvement. In 1986, TI appointed a new chief executive officer on the retirement of Ronald Utiger. The new CEO, Christopher Lewington, decided that TI needed a clear vision and strategy. Its acquisition strategy since the 1960s had been haphazard, to say the least, taking TI into a wide range of businesses that had no common thread. Early in 1987 he stated: 'TI's strategic task is to become an international engineering group concentrating on specialized engineering and operating in related markets on a global basis.'

Even at this stage, domestic appliances and cycles accounted for 42 per cent of group sales, 30 per cent of pre-tax profits and 45 per cent of capital employed. Despite strong emotional exit barriers, Raleigh bicycles was sold off and the whole of domestic appliances was quickly divested. Lewington felt that TI did not possess the financial resources nor the breadth of management necessary to run such a diversified spread of businesses covering both specialized engineering and consumer products and markets. Specialized engineering was where he thought TI could add value, gain significant returns and go global. Of course, strong brands in domestic appliances were snapped up by willing competitors, e.g. GEC, Birmid Qualcast and, ironically, given its demise in 1991, Polly-Peck. With the revenue generated, TI became an international player by acquisition. It established a strong presence in North America by purchasing Bundy, the largest US manufacturer of small diameter tube for use in cars and refrigerators and John Crane, a specialist manufacturer of mechanical seals. By 1991, TI's special engineering focus included aircraft piston rings, industrial furnaces and tubes for precisely defined market segments. TI has out-performed the industry consistently since it made these changes.

The lessons

1   A traditional portfolio analysis in 1986 would have suggested a retention of domestic appliances as a major cash cow and placed a large question mark or possible dog status over its specialized engineering businesses *at that time*. TI divested a successful part of its portfolio and rejuvenated a weaker part. By stepping back and taking stock of its future, it realized that domestic appliances could possibly face intense competition

over the medium term. Strength, however, could be had in specialized engineering niches world wide.

2   The sharp recovery in the early 1980s was due mainly to the heavy rationalization and to a smashing of the previous ways of 'doing business' with the introduction of fresh recipes brought in by a new chief executive officer. Its sustained success was also due to new ways of doing business brought in by its new chief executive, Christopher Lewington. One style of management being appropriate for recovery and one for sustaining the success.

3   Domestic markets were too restrictive for the type of specialized engineering that TI was involved in. Global, high value-added niches were essential to earn the high rates of return, with protection behind entry barriers. Seventy to 80 per cent of TI's international expansion in the later 1980s was accomplished by acquisition. This brought TI into existing networks with which it had little previous knowledge.

4   TI now concentrates on these precisely defined market niches that have an enduring quality throughout their maturity and eventual decline phases.

This organization then is clearly representative of all the best practice illustrated in Chapters 1, 2, 3 and 4. Its future performance and strategies should be worthy of observation.

If this book has one message it is that *we should think creatively before we decide to rely on automatic prescriptions of divestment for any low-share, low-growth businesses.*

Notes

Introduction

1 To define the unit of analysis, the remainder of the text will concentrate on businesses within the portfolio.
2 See, for instance, the work of Harrigan, Porter, Woo and Cooper, and of Grinyer and McKiernan, and Slatter.

1 Strategy formulation and the growth-share matrix

1 I am indebted to Professor Robin Wensley of the Warwick Business School, University of Warwick, for generous access to his personal correspondence with Bruce Henderson and Alan Zakon, to his previous research on the matrix and for helpful comments on this chapter. Any errors are mine.
2 Henderson (1988).
3 My emphasis.
4 See Francis J. Aguilar, *The Mead Corporation: Strategic Planning*, Boston: Harvard Business School, Case 9-379-070.
5 A crude formula can be built up to represent this maximum rate (Hax and Majluf 1984). If we assume that:

g = maximum sustainable growth (expressed as a yearly rate of increase of the equity base)
p = percentage of retained earnings
ROA = Post-tax return on Assets
D = Total debt
E = Total equity
i = Post-tax interest on debt
Total assets = $D + E$
Post tax returns are:

$$\Pi = (D + E)\ ROA - Di$$

or

$$\Pi = E.\ ROA + D\ (ROA - i)$$
$$\Pi = E.\ ROA + D\ (ROA - i)$$

The maximum rate of growth depends upon the amount of retained earnings. If p is equal to retained earnings over total earnings and g is the growth of equity then:

$$g = \frac{p.II}{E} = p \left[ROA + \frac{D}{E} (ROA - i) \right]$$

This is the maximum sustainable growth formula in simple terms. It assumes a constant D/E ratio and constant dividend policy as well as a fixed return on assets and cost of debt. It provides a guiding figure for growth at the corporate level.

6   Zakon remembers this as originally a 'wildcat' category although Wensley (1990) claims that Mead certainly used 'sweepstake'.
7   In 1973, Henderson claimed that 'such a single chart, with a projected position for five years out, is sufficient alone to tell a company's profitability, debt capacity, growth potential and competitive strength'.
8   For rigorous treatments see Wind (1982) and Hax and Majluf (1984; 1991).
9   Market growth, market share, sales and cash flow.
10   See Morrison and Wensley (1991), hereafter called the 'Warwick Survey'.
11   See, for example, Andrews and Brunner (1975).
12   It is even limited in its application to these structures – see discussion on p. 25, 'Time and change'.
13   See the commentary on p. 8, on the loss, in translation, of the risk-return pivot of financial portfolio theory.
14   In the original GE screen, the term 'business strengths' was used instead of competitive position. This was measured on a scale of high, medium, low. After Hofer and Schendel (1978) the term competitive position has been used, together with a scale of strong, average, weak, to bring it into line with discussions of the BCG matrix and other product/market evolution matrices.
15   Based on Walker (1990).
16   See case, copyright 1985 James Brian Quinn, with research associates Paquette, P.C. and Dixon, B. in 'Instructors' manual' to Quinn J.B., Mintzburg H. and James R.M., (1988) *The Strategy Process*, Englewood Press, NJ. Prentice Hall.

2   Corporate recovery

1   See, for instance Miles and Snow (1978); Hofer and Schendel (1978); Porter (1980; 1985); Chrisman, Hofer and Boulton (1988); Abell (1980); Kotler (1965).
2   The concept of relative decline is important. Companies in absolute decline have, by definition, an annual decrease in returns and are probably heading for failure in the short to medium term. Companies in relative decline need not be in absolute decline if their industry has a positive growth rate. For example, in an industry growing at 10 per cent p.a., a company is in relative decline with less than 10 per cent p.a. – say 8 per cent. Such a company may not face an annual depletion of

returns nor an extinction threat in the short to medium term.

3   This gradual change should be distinguished clearly from the incrementalism associated with the propositions of Lindblom (1959) or Quinn (1980).

4   I am indebted to Professor Peter Grinyer of the University of St Andrews Management Institute for providing significant theoretical structuring and commentary on this argument. A partial coverage of the model has appeared in the *Strategic Management Journal*, II, 1990, under our joint ownership. Any errors are mine.

5   See for example Hedberg, Nystrom and Starbuck (1976); Hedberg and Jonsson (1977); Grinyer and Spender (1979); Miller and Friesen (1984).

6   See Ansoff (1969): sequential versus parallel decision making.

7   See Grinyer, Mayes and McKiernan (1988).

3 Internationalization

1   Because the internationalization of business frequently starts with the product, some emphasis is placed on this unit of analysis during the chapter. However, as the chapter progresses, the emphasis falls back strongly upon the organization and so is consistent with the other chapters.

2   For social or political reasons, a state may attempt to achieve full employment by exporting all that it cannot consume domestically, perhaps due to the small size of its market. In other words, neo-mercantilism is a form of strategic 'breaking-out' from domestic market constraints on expansion.

3   The classicists categorized resources into land (natural resources), labour and capital but concentrated mostly on labour costs for the illustration of much of their work.

4   The analysis in this section is adapted from the exposition by Weekly and Aggarwal (1987).

5   Many items are held constant in this example to simplify the exposition, e.g. money and exchange rate, full employment, transport costs, mobility.

6   Hecksher-Ohlin theory of factor endowments.

7   In recent times, the mantle of product innovation has passed from the USA to Japan.

8   The strong basis for Hymer's work is the 'advantage' theory but, as Yamin (1991) has rightly stressed, Hymer made a second contribution which has virtually been ignored. The cases he examined in his thesis revolved around oligopolistic interdependence (US and British Tobacco firms in the 1950s) whose internationalization was not due solely to a specific advantage but to arrangements to remove conflict from their existing cut-throat competitiveness.

9   Arguably all of them can be traced to the seminal piece by Ronald Coase (1937), the 1991 Nobel Prize winner in Economics.

10   The argument in this section develops the original one by Forsgren (1989) for which I am indebted.

11 It is a separate debate as to what foreign means in such experienced international organizations.

4 Low-share/low-growth strategies in maturity and decline

1 The full approach is given in Chapter 9 of Hax and Majluf (1984).
2 See also Woo (1984) and Bourantas and Mandes (1987).
3 See Harrigan (1980).
4 The remainder of the section relies on the authoritative contributions of Harrigan (1980; 1982; 1988; 1990), Porter (1980) and Harrigan and Porter (1983).
5 IDR = (DE-DI) ÷ GBV where DE = depreciation of fixed assets in the year, DI = disposal of fixed assets in the year, GBV = gross book value of assets at the beginning of the year.
6 RCF = (DE-DI) + TE + P ÷ GBV where TE = tax equalization and P = profits

References

Abell, D.F. (1980) *Defining the Business: the Starting Point of Strategic Planning*, Englewood Cliffs, NJ: Prentice Hall.

Abell, D.F. and Hammond, J.S. (1979) *Strategic Market Planning*, New York: Prentice Hall.

Altman, E.L. (1968) 'Financial ratios: discriminant analysis and the prediction of corporate bankruptcy', *Journal of Finance* September, 23: 589–609.

Anderson, C.R. and Paine, F.T. (1978) 'PIMS: a re-examination', *Academy of Management Review* 3: 602–12.

Anderson, C.R. and Zeithaml, C.P. (1984) 'Stage of the product life cycle, business strategy, and business performance', *Academy of Management Journal* 27 (1): 5–24.

Andrews, K.R. (1981) 'Replaying the board's role in formulating strategy', *Harvard Business Review* May–June.

Andrews, P.W.S. and Brunner, E. (1975) *Studies in Pricing*, Basingstoke: Macmillan.

Ansoff, H.I. (1968) *Corporate Strategy*, Harmondsworth: Penguin.

—— (1969) 'Towards a strategic theory of the firm', in H.I. Ansoff (ed.) *Business Strategy*, Harmondsworth: Penguin.

—— (1984) *Implanting Strategic Management*, New York: Prentice Hall.

Argenti, J. (1976) *Corporate Collapse: the Causes and Symptoms*, Maidenhead, UK: McGraw Hill.

Baden Fuller, C.W.F, Dell'Osso, F. and Stopford, J.M. (1988), 'Competition dynamics behind the mask of maturity', discussion paper at the EIASM Conference, Brussels, November 1988.

Bain, J.S. (1956) *Barriers to New Competition*, Cambridge, Mass.: Harvard University Press.

Baumol, W.J., Panzar, J.C. and Willig, R.D. (1982) *Contestable Markets and the Theory of Industry Structure*, New York: Harcourt Brace Jovanovich.

Berle, A.A. and Means, G. (1932) *The Modern Corporation and Private Property*, New York: Macmillan.

Bibeault, D.B. (1982) *Corporate Turnaround: How Managers Turn Losers into Winners*, New York: McGraw Hill.

Bilkey, W. and Tesar, G. (1977) 'The export behaviour of smaller Wisconsin manufacturing firms', *Journal of International Business Studies* spring–summer, 93–8.

Biteman, J. (1979) 'Turnaround management: an exploratory study of rapid total organisation change', doctoral dissertation, Harvard University, quoted in Hoffman op. cit.

Bourantas, D. and Mandes, Y. (1987) 'Does market share lead to profitability?' *Long Range Planning* 20 (5): 102–8.

Bowman, E.H. (1974) 'Epistemology, corporate strategy and academe', *Sloan Management Review*, winter.

Branson, W.H. and Monoyios, N. (1977) 'Factor inputs in US trade', *Journal of International Economics* May, 7: 111–31.

Brookes, M.R. and Rosson, P.J. (1982) 'A study of export behaviour of small and medium sized manufacturing firms in three Canadian provinces', in M.R. Czinkota and G. Tesar (eds.) *Export Management: an International Context*, New York: Praeger.

Buckley, P.J. (1983) 'New theories of international business, some unresolved issues', in Mark C. Casson (ed.) *The Growth of International Business*, London: Allen & Unwin.

Buckley, P.J. and Casson, M. (1976) *The Future of the Multinational Enterprise*, London: Macmillan.

Burns, T. and Stalker, G.M. (1961) *The Management of Innovation*, London: Tavistock.

Buzzell, R. (1966) 'Competitive behaviour and product life cycles', in J.S. Wright and J.L. Goldstucker (eds) *New Ideas for Successful Marketing*, Chicago: American Marketing Association.

Buzzell, R., Gale, B. and Sultan, R. (1975), 'Market share: a key to profitability', *Harvard Business Review* 53 (1):: 97–106.

Cameron, K.S., Sutton, R.I. and Whetten, D.A. (eds) (1988) *Readings in Organisational Decline: 'Frameworks, research and prescriptions'*, Cambridge, Mass.: Barringer Publishing Company.

Casson, M.C. (1982) 'Transaction costs and the theory of the multinational enterprise', in Alan M. Rugman (ed.), *New Theories of the Multinational Enterprise*, New York: St Martin's Press.

Caves, R.E. (1971) 'International corporations: the industrial economics of foreign investment', *Economica*: 1–27.

—— (1982) *Multinational Enterprise and Economic Analysis*, New York: Cambridge University Press.

Cavusgil, S.T. (1982) 'Some observations on the relevance of critical variables for internationalisation stages' in M.R. Czinkota and G. Tesar (eds), *Export Management: an International Context*, New York: Praeger.

Cavusgil, S.T. and Nevin, J.R. (1980) 'A conceptualization of the initial involvement in international marketing', in C.W. Lamb Jnr. and P.M. Dunne (eds) *Theoretical Development in Marketing*, New York: American Marketing Association.

Chrisman, J., Hofer, C. and Boulton, W.R. (1988) 'Towards a system for classifying business strategies', *Academy of Management Review* 13 (3): 413–28.

Clark, P. (1979) 'Cultural context as a determinant of organisational rationality', in C. Lammers and D. Hickson (eds) *Organisations Alike and Unalike: International and Inter-Institutional Studies in the Sociology of Organisations*, London: Routledge.

Clark, P. and Starkey, K. (1988) *Organisation, Transition and Innovation Design*, London: Pinter.

Clifford, D.J. Jnr. (1977), 'Managing the product life cycle', in R. Mann (ed.) *The Arts of Top Management: a McKinsey Anthology*, New York: McGraw Hill.

Coase, R.H. (1937) 'The nature of the firm', *Economica* November, 4: 386–405.

Cox, W.F. (1967), 'Product life cycles as marketing models', *Journal of Business* October, 40: 375–84.

Cunningham, N.T. and Culligan, K. (1991), 'Competitiveness through networks of relationships in information technology product markets', in S.J. Paliwoda *New Perspectives on International Marketing*, London: Routledge.

Cyert, R.M. and March, J.G. (1963) *A Behavioural Theory of the Firm*, Englewood Cliffs, New York: Prentice Hall.

Czinkota, M.R., Rivolt, P. and Ronkainen, I.A. (1989) *International Business*, New York: Dryden Press, Holt, Rhinehart and Winston.

Daniels, J.D. and Radebaugh, L.H. (1988) *International Business: Environments and Operations*, 5th edn, Reading, Mass.: Addison-Wesley.

Day, G.S. (1977) 'Diagnosing the product portfolio', *Journal of Marketing* April, 29–38.

—— (1981) 'The product life cycle: analysis and application issues', *Journal of Marketing* Fall.

Dhalla, N.K. and Yuspeth, S. (1976), 'Forget the product life cycle concept', *Harvard Business Review* January–February, 54: 102–12.

Dichtl, L.E.M., Liebold, M., Koglmayr, H.G. and Muller, S. (1983) 'The foreign orientation of management as a central construct in export centred decision making processes', *Research for Marketing* 10: 7–14.

Doyle, P. (1976), 'The realities of the product life cycle', *Quarterley Review of Marketing* summer, 1–6.

Dunning, J.H. (1981) *International Production and the Multinational Enterprise*, London: Allen & Unwin.

Dunning, J.H. and Rugman, A.M. (1985) 'The influence of Hymer's dissertation on the theory of foreign direct investment', *AEA Papers and Proceedings* May, 75 (2): 228–32.

Easton, G. and Lundgren (1991) 'Changes in industrial networks as flow through notes', in S.J. Paliwoda (ed.) *New Perspectives in International Marketing*, London: Routledge.

Ford, D. and Leonidou, L. (1991) 'Research developments in international marketing: a European perspective', in S.J. Paliwoda (ed.) *New Perspectives on International Marketing*, London: Routledge.

Ford, I.D., Lawson, A. and Nicholls, J.R. (1982) 'Developing international marketing through overseas sales subsidiaries', in M.R. Czinkota and G. Tesar (eds) *Export Management: An International Context*, New York: Praeger.

Forsgren, M. (1989) *Managing the Internationalisation Process: a Swedish Case*, London: Routledge.

Forsgren, M. and Johanson, J. (1975) *Internationell foretagsekonomi* Stockholm: Norstedts.

Forsstrom, B. (1991) 'Competitive distribution networks: the Finnish magazine industry in the UK', in S.J. Paliwoda (ed.) *New Perspectives in International Marketing*, London: Routledge.

Friberg, E. (1988) 'The challenge of 1992', *McKinsey Quarterly* autumn.

Friedmann, R. and Kimm, J. (1988) 'Political risk and international marketing', *Columbia Journal of World Business* winter.

Fruhan, W.E. (1972) 'Pyrrhic victories in fights for market share', *Harvard Business Review* October, 50.

Galbraith, C. and Schendel, D.E. (1982), 'A life cycle model of business strategy', working paper, University of California, Urvin: Graduate School of Management.

Ghoshals (1987) 'Global strategy: an organising framework', *Strategic Management Journal* 8: 425–40.

Goold, M. (1981) 'Why dicey definitions are so dangerous', *Financial Times* 16 November 1981.

Grinyer, P.H. (1971) 'The anatomy of business strategy planning reconsidered', *Journal of Management Studies* 8 (3): 199–212.

Grinyer, P.H. and McKiernan, P. (1990) 'Generating major change in stagnating companies', *Strategic Management Journal* 11: 131–46.

—— (1991), 'Simultaneous equation model of profitability and growth', working paper, University of Warwick: Warwick Business School.

—— (forthcoming) 'Typologies of corporate recovery', in P. Barrar and C. Cooper (eds) *Management in the 1990s*, London: Routledge.

—— (1992 forthcoming) Corporate growth: single and simultaneous equation determination', *British Academy of Management Journal.*

Grinyer, P.H. and Spender, J.C. (1979) *Turnaround: Managerial Recipes for Strategic Success*, London: Associated Business Publications.

Grinyer, P.H., Mayes, D. and McKiernan, P. (1988) *Sharpbenders: the Secrets of Unleashing Corporate Potential*, Oxford: Basil Blackwell.

Hakansson, H. (1982) *International Marketing and Purchasing of Industrial Goods: an Interaction Approach*, London: John Wiley.

Hall, W.K. (1982), 'Survival strategies in a hostile environment', *McKinsey Quarterly* winter, 2–22.

Hallen, L., Johanson, J. and Seyed Mohamad, N. (1987) 'Relationship strength and stability in international and domestic industrial marketing', *Industrial Marketing and Purchasing* 2 (3): 22–37.

Hambrick, D.C. and D'Aveni R.A. (1988) 'Large corporate failures as downward spirals', *Administrative Science Quarterly* March, 33: 1–23.

Hambrick, D.C. and Schecter, S.M. (1983) 'Turnaround strategies for mature industrial product business units', *Academy of Management Journal* 26 (2): 231–48.

Hambrick, D.C., MacMillan, I.C. and Day, D.L. (1982) 'Strategic attributes and performance in the BCG matrix: a PIMS-based analysis of industrial product business', *Academy of Management Journal* September.

Hamermesh, R.G. and Silk, S.B. (1979) 'How to compete in stagnant industries', *Harvard Business Review* September–October, 161–8.

Hamermesh, R.G., Anderson, M.J. and Harris, J.E. (1978) 'Strategies for low market share businesses', *Harvard Business Review* 56 (3): 95–102.

Harrigan, K.R. (1980), 'Strategies for declining businesses', *Journal of Business Strategy* fall, 20–34.

—— (1982), 'Strategic planning for end game', *Long Range Planning* 15 (6): 45–8.

—— (1988), *Managing Mature Businesses*, Lexington, Mass.: D.C. Heath & Co.

—— (1990), 'Will you be the last iceman', *Sales and Marketing Management* 142 (1): 62–7.

Harrigan, K.R. and Porter, M.E. (1983) 'End game strategies for declining industries', *Harvard Business Review* July–August, 111–20.

Haspeslagh, P. (1982) 'Portfolio planning: uses and limits', *Harvard Business Review* January–February.

Hax, A. and Majluf, N.S. (1984) *Strategic Management: An Integrative Perspective*, Englewood Cliffs, NJ.: Prentice Hall (2nd edn 1991).

Hecksher, E. (1919) 'The effect of foreign trade on the distribution of income', *Economist Tidskrift* 21: 497–512.

Hedberg, B., Nystrom, P.C. and Starbuck, W. (1976) 'Camping on seasaws: prescriptions for a self designing organisation', *Administrative Science Quarterly* 21 (1): 41–65.

Hedberg, B. and Jonsson, S.A. (1977) 'Strategy formulation as a discontinuous process', *International Studies of Management and Organisation* 7 (2): 88–109.

Hedley, B. (1977) 'Strategy and the business portfolio', *Long Range Planning*, February 10: 9–15.

Henderson, B. (1970) 'The product portfolio', *BCG Perspectives* 66.

—— (1973) 'The experience curve reviewed: the growth share matrix or the product portfolio', *BCG Perspectives* 135.

—— (1979) *Henderson on Corporation Strategy*, Cambridge, Mass.: Abt. Books.

—— (1988) 'Private correspondence with R. Wensley', Warwick University: Warwick Business School.

Hennart, J.H. (1982) *A Theory of Multinational Enterprise*, Ann Arbour University of Michigan Press.

Hewitt, G. (1988) unpublished lecture, Barclays Bank Seminar, 14 July, quoted in Morrison and Wensley, op. cit.

Hickson, D.J., Butler, R.J., Cray, D., Mallory, G.R. and Wilson, D.C. (1986) *Top Decisions: Strategic Decision Making In Organizations*, Oxford: Blackwell; San Francisco: Jossey-Bass.

Hofer, C.W. (1977) *Conceptual Constructs for Formulating Corporate and Businesses Strategies*, Boston: Intercollegiate Case Clearing House, No. 9-378-754), p. 3.

—— (1980) 'Turnaround strategies', *Journal of Business Strategy* 1 (1): 19–31.

Hofer, C.W. and Schendel, D.E. (1978) *Strategy Formulation: Analytical Concepts*, St Paul: West Publishing.

Hoffman, R.C. (1989) 'Strategies for corporate turnarounds: what do we know about them?' *Journal of General Management* spring, 14 (3): 46–66.

Howe, W.S. (1986) *Corporate Strategy*, Basingstoke: Macmillan.

Hughes, K. (1982) 'Corporate response to declining rates of growth', Lexington Books, Mass.: D.C. Heath & Co.

Hutton, J. (1988) *The World of the International Manager*, Oxford: Philip Allan.

Hymer, S.H. (1960) *The International Operations of National Firms: A Study of Direct Foreign Investment*, Cambridge: MIT Press.

Jatar, A. (1992) unpublished PhD dissertation, 'Vertical integration and control of distribution channels: the case of Venezuela', Warwick University of Warwick.

Johanson, J. and Vahlne, J. (1977) 'The internationalisation process of the firm: a model of knowledge development on increasing foreign commitments', *Journal of International Business Studies* spring–summer, 23–32.

Johanson, J. and Wiedersheim-Paul, F. (1975) 'The internationalisation of the firm: four Swedish case studies', *Journal of Management Studies* October, 305–22.

Joynt, P. (1982) 'An empirical study of Norwegian export behaviour', in M.R. Czinkota and G. Tesar (eds), *Export Management: an International Context*, New York: Praeger.

Julius, D. (1990) reported in the *Financial Times*, December.

Kay, N.M. (1983) 'Multinational enterprises: a review article', *Scottish Journal of Political Economy* 30 (3): 304–12.

Kenen, P.B. (1965) 'Nature capital and trade', *Journal of Political Economy* October, 73: 437–60.

Kern, D. (1985) 'The evaluation of country risk and economic potential', *Long Range Planning* 18 (3): 17–25.

Kotler, P. (1965) 'Competitive strategies for new product marketing for the life cycle', *Mangement Science*, December, 12: B104–B119.

—— (1984) *Marketing Management: analysis, planning and control*, 5th edn, Englewood Cliffs, New Jersey: Prentice Hall.

Lawrence, P.R. and Lorsch, J.D. (1967) *Organization and Environment Division of Research*, Harvard, Harvard Business School.

Lee, W. and Brasch, J.J. (1978) 'The adoption of export as an innovative strategy', *Journal of International Business Studies* spring–summer, 85–93.

Leontief, W.W. (1954) 'Domestic production and foreign trade: the American capital position re-examined', *Economia Internazionale* February, 7: 3–34.

Levitt, T. (1960) 'Marketing myopia', *Harvard Business Review* July–August, 45–56.

—— (1965) 'Exploit the product life cycle', *Harvard Business Review* November–December, 81–94.

Lindblom, C.E. (1959) 'The science of muddling through', *Public Administration Review*, 79–88.

Linder, S. (1961) *An Essay on Trade and Transformation*, New York: John Wiley.

Lorenz, C. (1981) 'Why Boston recounted its doctrine of market leadership', *Financial Times*, 20 November.

Lorange, P. (1975) 'Divisional planning: setting effective direction', *Sloan Management Review*, fall.

Lorange, P. and Vancil, R. (1977) *Strategic Planning Systems*, Englewood Cliffs, NJ.: Prentice Hall.

Lutz, J.M. and Green, R.T. (1983) 'The product lifecycle and the export position of the United States', *Journal of International Business Studies* winter, 77–93.

McNamee, P. (1988) *Management Accounting: Strategic Planning and Marketing*, Oxford: Heinemann.

Majaro, S. (1977) 'Market share: deception or diagnosis', *Marketing* March.

Markowitz, H.M. (1952) 'Portfolio selection', *Journal of Finance* March, 77–91.

Mascarenhas, B. and Aaker, D.A. (1989) 'Strategy over the business cycle', *Strategic Management Journal* 10: 119–210.

Mattsson, L.G. (1986) 'Indirect relations in industrial networks: a conceptual analysis of their strategic significance', paper presented at the 3rd IMP Research Seminar on International Marketing, Lyons, quoted in Cunningham and Culligan op. cit.

Melin, L. (1985) 'Strategies in managing turnaround', *Long Range Planning* 18 (1): 80–6.

Miles, R. and Snow, C. (1978) *Organisational Strategy, Structure and Process*, New York: McGraw Hill.

Miles, R.E. and Snow, C.C. (1986) 'Organisations: new concepts for new forms', *California Management Review* 28: 62–73.

Mill, J.S. (1848) *Principles of Political Economy*, London: Longmans Green.

Miller, D. and Friesen, P.H. (1984) *Organisations: a Quantum Leap*, Englewood Cliffs, NJ: Prentice Hall.

Mintzberg, H. (1983) *Structure in Firms: Designing Effective Organisations*, Englewood Cliffs, NJ: Prentice Hall.

—— (1988) 'Opening up the definition of strategy', in J.B. Quin, H. Mintzberg and R.M. James (eds) *The Strategy Process: Concepts, Contexts and Cases*, Englewood Cliffs, NJ: Prentice Hall.

Morrison, A. and Wensley, R. (1991) 'Boxing up or boxed-in?: a short history of the Boston Consulting Group share/growth matrix', *Journal of Marketing Management*.

Nadler, D.A. and Tushman, M.L. (1989) 'Organisational framebending: principles for managing reorientation', *Academy of Management Executive*, 3 (3): 194–204.

Ohlin, B. (1933) *Interregional and International Trade*, Cambridge, Mass.: Harvard University Press.

Ohmae (1990) *The Borderless World: Power and Strategy in the Interlinked Economy*, London: Collins.

Olson, H.C. and Wiedersheim-Paul, F. (1978) 'Factors affecting the pre-export behaviour of non-exporting firms', in J. Leontiades (ed.) *European Research in International Business*, Amsterdam: North Holland.

O'Neill, H.M. (1986) 'Turnaround and recovery: what strategy do you need?', *Long Range Planning* 19 (1): 80–8.

Perlitz, M. (1985) 'Country portfolio analysis: assessing country risk and opportunity', *Long Range Planning* 18 (4): 11–26.

Pettigrew, A.M. and Whipp, R. (1990) 'Leading change and the management of competition', paper presented to the Cranfield Strategic Management Society Workshop: Leadership and the Management of Strategic Change, Cambridge: University of Cambridge, 11–14 December.

—— (1991) *Managing Change for Competitive Success* Oxford: Basil Blackwell.

Pfeffer, J. (1978) *Organisational Design*, Arlington Heights, Illinois: AHM.
Pitelis, C.N. and Sugden, R. (1991) *The Nature of the Transnational Firm*, London: Routledge.
Pondy, L. (1984) 'Union of rationality and intuition in management action', in Shrivastava and associates (eds) *The Executive Mind: New Insights on Managerial Thought and Action*, San Francisco: Jossey-Bass.
Porter, M.E. (1980) *Competitive Strategy Techniques for Analysing Industries and Competitors*, New York: Free Press.
—— (1985) *Competitive Advantage: Creating and Sustaining Superior Performance*, New York: Free Press.
—— (1986) 'Changing patterns of international competition', *California Management Review* winter, 28 (2): 9–39.
—— (1990) *The Competitive Advantage of Nations*, London: Macmillan.
Quinn, J.B. (1980) *Strategies for Change: Logical Incrementalism*, Homewood, Ill.: Richard D. Irwin.
Rafferty, J. (1987) 'Exit barriers and strategic position in declining markets', *Long Range Planning* 20 (2): 86–91.
Ramanujam, V. (1984) 'Environmental Organisational context: strategy and corporate turnaround', doctoral dissertation, Pittsburgh: University of Pittsburgh, cited in Hoffman op. cit.
Ricardo, D. (1817) *Principles of Political Economy and Taxation*, London: J.M. Dent & Sons.
Rink, D. and Swan, J. (1979) 'Product life cycle research: a literature review', *Journal of Business Research* 7: 219–42.
Robinson, S.J.Q. (1986) 'Strategies for declining industrial markets', *Long Range Planning* 19 (2): 72–8.
Rugman, A.M. (1981) *Inside the Multinationals: the Economics of Internal Markets*, New York: Columbia University Press.
—— (1986) 'New theories of the multinational enterprise: an assessment of internalization theory' *Bulletin of Economic Research* 38 (2): 101–18.
—— (ed.) (1982) *New Theories of the Multinational Enterprise*, New York: St Martin's Press.
Rugman, A.M. and Verbeke, A. (1991) *Global Corporate Strategy and Trade Policy*, London: Routledge.
Rumelt, R.P. and Wensley, R. (1981) 'In search of the market share effect', proceedings of the Academy of Management, 41st annual meeting, San Diego, pp. 2–6.
Schendel, D.E., Patten, and Riggs, J. (1976) 'Corporate turnaround strategies: a study of profit decline and recovery', *Journal of General Management* 3: 3–11.
Scherer, F.M. (1980) *Industrial Market Structure and Economic Performance*, 2nd edn, Chicago: Rand McNally.
Scherer, F.M. and Ross, D. (1990) *Industrial Market Structure and Economic Performance*, 3rd edn, Boston, Mass.: Houghton Mifflin.
Schoeffler, S., Buzzell, R. and Heany, D. (1974) 'Impact of strategic planning on profit performance', *Harvard Business Review* March–April, 52 (2).
Schofield, M. and Arnold, D. (1988) 'Strategies for mature businesses', *Long Range Planning* 21 (5): 69–76.
Simmonds, K. and Smith, H. (1968) 'The first export order: a marketing

innovation', *British Journal of Marketing* summer, 93–100.

Simpson, C.L. Jnr and Kujawa, D. (1974) 'The export decision process: an empirical enquiry', *Journal of International Business Studies* spring, 107–17.

Slatter, S. (1980) 'Common pitfalls in using the BCG product portfolio matrix', *London Business School Journal* winter, 18–22.

—— (1984) *Corporate Recovery*, Harmondsworth: Penguin.

Smith, A. (1776) *An Enquiry into the Nature and Causes of the Wealth of Nations*, New York: The Modern Library (1937).

Smith, K.G., Mitchell, T.R. and Summer, C.E. (1985) 'Top level management priorities in different stages of the organisational life cycle', *Academy of Management Journal* 28 (4): 799–820.

Solberg, C.A. (1988) 'Successful and unsuccessful exporters: a study of 114 Norwegian export companies', Norwegian School of Management working paper 1988/27.

—— (1989) 'Responding to the globalisation challenge: suggestive framework for analysis and decision making', paper presented to the 1990 EIASM workshop on global strategic management, spring (1990).

Spender, J.C. (1979) 'Strategy making in business', unpublished PhD thesis, Manchester: Manchester Business School.

Starbuck, W.H., Greve, A. and Hedberg, B.L.T. (1978) 'Responding to crises', *Journal of Business Administration* spring, 111–78.

Stobaugh, R.B. (1969) 'How to analyse foreign investment climates', *Harvard Business Review* September–October, 100–108.

Stopford, J.M. and Baden-Fuller, C. (1990) 'Corporate rejuvenation', paper given at the EIASM Conference in Strategic Management, winter.

Teece, D.J. (1981) 'Multinational enterprises: market failure and market power considerations', *Sloan Management Review* 22 (3): 3–17.

—— (1985) 'Transactions cost economics and the multinational enterprise: an assessment', *Barclay International Business Working Paper Series*, No. IB-3.

Tesar, G. (1975) 'Empirical study of export operations among small and medium sized manufacturing firms', unpublished PhD dissertation, Madison: University of Wisconsin.

Tesar, G. and Tarleton, J.S. (1982) 'Comparison of Wisconsin and Virginian small and medium sized exporters: aggressive and passive exporters', in M.R. Czinkota and G. Tesar (eds) *Export Management: An International Context*, New York: Praeger.

Thietart, R.A. and Vivas, R. (1984) 'An empirical investigation of success strategies for businesses along the product life cycle', *Management Science* 30 (12): 1405–22.

Thompson, A.A. Jnr. and Strickland, III, A.J. (1990) 'Strategic Management: Concepts and Cases, Boston, Mass.: BPI/Urwin.

Thompson, J.L. (1990) *Strategic Management: Awareness and Changes*, London: Chapman and Hall.

Thorelli, H.B. (1986) 'Networks: between markets and hierarchies', *Strategic Management Journal* 7: 37–51.

Tinsley, T. (1986) *Interpreting the Drive Towards Globalization in Shaping Respective Responses to the Globalization Challenge*, New York: McKinsey.

Vernon, R. (1966) 'International investment and international trade in the product cycle', *Quarterly Journal of Economics* May, 80: 190–207.

Vesper, V.D. (1983) 'Letter to briefcase', *Long Range Planning* 16: 119.

Walker, R. (1990) 'Analysing the business portfolio in Black and Decker Europe', in Taylor, B. and Harrison, J. (eds) *The Manager's Casebook of Business Strategy*, Oxford: Heinemann.

Weekly, J.K. and Aggarwal, R. (1987) *International Business: Operating in the Global Economy* New York: The Dryden Press.

Welch, L.S. and Wiedersheim-Paul, F. (1980) 'Initial exports: a marketing failure query', *Journal of Management Studies* October, 333–44.

Wensley, R. (1981) 'Strategic marketing: betas, boxes or basics', *Journal of Marketing* summer, 45: 173–82.

—— (1987) Chapters 6 and 7, Warwick: University of Warwick Distance Learning MBA Study Notes.

—— (1990) 'Private correspondence with A. Zakon', Warwick: Warwick Business School.

Whetten, D.A. (1987) 'Organisational growth and decline processes', *Annual Review of Sociology* 13: 333–58.

Whipp, R., Rosenfield, R. and Pettigrew, A. (1989) 'Managing strategic change in a mature business', *Long Range Planning* 22 (6): 92–9.

Wiedersheim-Paul, F., Olson, H.C. and Welch, L.S. (1978) 'Pre-export activity: the first step in internationalisation', *Journal of International Business Studies* spring–summer, 47–58.

Williamson, O.E. (1975) *Markets and Hierarchies: Analysis and Antitrust Implications: a Study of the Economics of Internal Organisations*, New York: Free Press.

Wilson, A. and Atkin, B. (1976) 'Exorcising the ghosts in marketing', *Harvard Business Review* Sept–October, 54.

Wilson, D.C. (1992) *A Strategy of Change: Concepts and Controversies in the Management of Change*, London: Routledge Series in Analytical Management.

Wind, Y.J. (1982) *Product Policy: Concepts, Methods and Strategy*, Reading, Mass.: Addison-Wesley.

Wind, Y. and Mahajan, V.J. (1981) 'Designing a product and business portfolios', *Harvard Business Review* January–February, 59.

Wind, Y., Mahajan, V.J. and Swire, D.J. (1981) 'Standardized portfolio models: an empirical comparison of business classifications', proceedings of MSI conference or analytical approaches to product and marketing planning, October.

Woo, C.Y. (1984) 'Market-share leadership: not always so good', *Harvard Business Review* January–February, 53–4.

Woo, C.Y.Y. and Cooper, A.C. (1981) 'Strategies of effective low share businesses', *Strategic Management Journal* 2: 301–18.

Wright, R.V.L. (1971) *Strategy Centres: a Contemporary Managing System*, Cambridge, Mass.: Arthur D. Little.

Yamin, M. (1991) 'A reassessment of Hymer's contribution to the theory of the transnational firm', in C.M. Pitelis and R. Sugden (eds) *The Nature of the Transnational Firm*, London: Routledge.

Zimmerman, F.M. (1986) 'Turnaround: a painful learning experience', *Long Range Planning* 19 (4): 104–14.

—— (1989) 'Managing a successful turnaround', *Long Range Planning* 22 (3): 105–24.

Index